iPhone®
MADE EASY

This is a FLAME TREE book
First published 2015

Publisher and Creative Director: Nick Wells
Project Editor: Polly Prior
Art Director and Layout Design: Mike Spender
Digital Design and Production: Chris Herbert
Copy Editor: Daniela Nava
Technical Editor: Mark Mayne
Screenshots: Chris Smith

Special thanks to: Josie Mitchell, Helen Snaith and Dawn Laker.

This edition first published 2015 by
FLAME TREE PUBLISHING
Crabtree Hall, Crabtree Lane
Fulham, London SW6 6TY
United Kingdom

www.flametreepublishing.com

15 17 19 18 16
1 3 5 7 9 10 8 6 4 2

ISBN 978-1-78361-326-7

A CIP record for this book is available from the British Library upon request.

Printed in China

All non-screenshot pictures are © 2013 Apple Inc.: 8, 9, 10, 21, 154, 234; and imore.com: 25; and news.cnet.com: 196; and iStock
and © the following photographers: pressureUA: 5, 94; Erikona: 5, 54; georgeclerk: 6, 166; Onfokus: 6, 152; BlueMoonPics: 20, 208;
tamergunal: 22; CatLane: 164; and Shutterstock and © the following photographers: Denys Prykhodov: 4, 7, 12, 128, 134, 218;
successo images: 9; Ostancov Vladislav: 18; Oleg GawriloFF 19, 75, 81; NorGal: 24; nenetus: 47; hitmanphoto: 50; Ekaterina_Minaeva:
62; Sebastian Gauert: 72; Zeynep Demir: 84, 85; tulpahn: 100; Chukcha: 118; Pressmaster: 156; leonardo2011 159; blvdone: 163, 195,
225; alexisdc: 185; eljkodan: 191; guteksk7: 228; Hadrian: 246. All other images courtesy of Flame Tree Publishing Ltd.

5C 5S 6
iPhone®
MADE EASY

KIERAN ALGER AND CHRIS SMITH

FLAME TREE
PUBLISHING

CONTENTS

It's often difficult to know where to start if you have never used an iPhone before. This chapter will introduce what you can accomplish with your new smartphone; it will also furnish you with the knowledge needed to get past the initial setup process and to get comfortable with the device. You'll become accustomed to using the touch screen, moving around the iOS software, opening apps and accessing some of the iPhone's basic features.

USING THE iPHONE **54**

Although the iPhone is a multifunctional device, harnessing the power of several gadgets rolled into one, at its core it is still a communications tool. This chapter offers a comprehensive guide to making and receiving phone calls, setting up voicemail, importing your contacts, sending and receiving text and picture messages, and even video chatting with your friends and family.

GETTING CONNECTED **94**

With the iPhone, the entire world is in your pocket. In this chapter, you'll learn how to browse the internet using the Safari app, send and receive email, control your calendar, and post updates to Facebook and Twitter. This chapter will also explain in foolproof detail how to use the iPhone's powerful location services, which allow you to summon directions instantly, check in at your favourite restaurant, find nearby attractions and explore cities new and old.

APPS 152

The mobile apps phenomenon was pioneered by the iPhone, and in this chapter, we'll learn how to download and make use of these new and exciting tools from the Apple App Store and we'll discover how they can be used to keep your iPhone feeling fresh and new every single day.

MULTIMEDIA 166

This chapter features a comprehensive guide to taking great pictures and video, and sharing them with your friends and family; we'll also explore how to acquire and play your favourite games, music, movies and TV shows, how to read books and magazines, and how to improve your lifestyle through a host of dedicated apps and services.

ADVANCED iPHONE 218

Need to restore from a backup? Improve your battery life? Make use of online file storage apps? It's all here. This chapter also features a detailed troubleshooting guide to counter some of the common problems you'll come across when using your iPhone.

INTRODUCTION

As you're reading this book, you've probably just become the lucky owner of a brand new iPhone. Now the iPhone is in your hands, you may be wondering what to do with it. This book offers both a practical and educational guide to quickly mastering this pocket-size marvel of modern technology.

Above: The iPhone is many devices rolled into one, plus so much more.

WHAT CAN I DO WITH AN iPHONE?

The iPhone boasts an incredible number of practical everyday tools for personal and business use. It encompasses a multitude of modern devices but is still small enough to fit in the palm of your hand. It's a phone, a personal organizer, a music and video player, a camera and so much more. This book will help you to master simple tasks, such as making phone calls and sending emails, to more complex tasks, such as taking photos, using apps to edit them and then logging on to the internet in order to upload them to your favourite social networks.

A QUICK iPHONE HISTORY LESSON

There have been 10 versions of the iPhone. While this book focuses on the newer models, the iPhone 5C, 5S, 6 and 6 Plus, many of the features described apply to the older models, and so if a particular aspect only applies to newer or older handsets, we'll make that clear. Here's a brief guide to the features and improvements each handset offered down the years.

iPhone Models

Here's a summary of each new version of the iPhone to date:

- **iPhone (2007):** The first iPhone featured a web browser, an integrated iPod music player, a video player and dedicated applications (apps) such as Weather, Calendar and Google Maps.

- **iPhone 3G (2008):** The second coming brought a faster 3G internet and better GPS. The App Store was also introduced, bringing new web-based applications and games.

- **iPhone 3GS (2009):** The third iPhone brought a host of speed improvements and included a compass, voice control and a slightly improved camera.

- **iPhone 4 (2010):** The iPhone 4 had a critically acclaimed stainless-steel and glass design, a 5-megapixel camera, a front-facing camera for video calls and the new high-resolution Retina display.

- **iPhone 4S (2011):** The iPhone 4S introduced Siri – a voice-controlled personal assistant – and an online backup solution called iCloud. The camera was boosted to 8 megapixels with full high-definition video recording.

- **iPhone 5 (2012):** This had a larger screen, more power, better graphics, super-fast fourth-generation mobile internet (4G LTE) and a new charging/syncing connector.

- **iPhone 5S (2013):** No design overhaul here, but Apple added the Touch ID fingerprint sensor, shoring up the security.

Right: Side view of the sleek iPhone 5S.

Above: The colourful iPhone 5C with a protective case.

- **iPhone 5C (2013):** In response to demand for a more affordable iPhone, Apple launched the iPhone 5C. It retained the specs of the iPhone 5, but gave the handset a colourful plastic coating.

- **iPhone 6 (2014):** A design overhaul and a larger screen, the iPhone 6 got slimmer, lighter and rounder integrating a 4.7-inch screen. iOS 8 also arrived with this handset.

- **iPhone 6 Plus (2014):** This is Apple's largest handset yet, at 5.5 inches; it is also the first iPhone to boast a full HD 1080p screen.

Apple iOS Software

You'll read a lot about iOS in this book: it's the software that comes preloaded on to the iPhone for use straight out of the box. The latest version is iOS 8, which the majority of iPhone owners are now using, while almost all of the rest are on iOS 7. Apple's improvements to its iPhone handsets each year are always accompanied by a tweaked version of iOS, but even if you're

Above: The iPhone 6 (left) and 6 Plus (right) models have bigger screens than their predecessors, as well as improved cameras.

using an older phone (4S and up), you can still upgrade to the new software every time. When certain features are only available in iOS 8, we'll make that clear.

DIVE IN AND DIVE OUT

This book has been written in the hope that you will dive in and out when you need a helping hand to understand a particular feature or if you're having trouble overcoming a problem. For example, if you don't know how to download music from iTunes, or email a picture, you can head straight to that page for a detailed explanation. If you're stumped, the easiest thing to do is to look up your topic in the index page.

JARGON BUSTING

While we have made every effort to crush buzzwords and display instructions in the simplest possible terms, sometimes jargon is unavoidable when describing features (iTunes Syncing, iCloud Photo Streams, etc.).

Above: The book contains useful screenshots that help you understand what is being explained.

HELP!

We are very confident that the information within this book can help you to become fluent in the language of iPhone in no time at all. However, if you need further advice, help is always close by. The Apple Support website offers hugely detailed archives on how to master each feature and overcome problems.

Hot Tips

Throughout the book, we have inserted a host of Hot Tips to help you get the most out of your iPhone. These simple features can be less obvious or hidden away, but can provide the key to unlocking more cool features on your iPhone handset.

GETTING STARTED

WHAT IS AN iPHONE?

An iPhone is a mobile phone with software that lets users search the internet, send email, play music, video and games, take photos, shoot video and find directions. Here, we'll introduce some of the key uses for your new iPhone: there are more than you think!

Above: Once an active SIM card has been installed, the iPhone can be used to make and receive calls.

COMMUNICATION

Multi-talented the iPhone may be, but its primary function is still communication. Here are some of the ways you can use it to keep in touch directly with friends and family; all will be explained in more detail throughout this book.

Phone

Once an active SIM card is placed in the device, you'll be able to make and receive calls by pressing the Phone icon on the device's Home screen and using the onscreen dial pad.

Messaging

The SMS (short message service) or 'texting' app is a primary function of the iPhone. Messages are typed on the touch-screen keypad and, once sent, will appear in a thread, allowing you to keep track of conversations over time. iPhone, iPad, Mac and iPod touch owners can exchange messages with each other for free over Wi-Fi or mobile internet using Apple's own iMessage service.

Email

The iPhone's native email app allows you to send and receive electronic mail directly to your handset; it's easy to configure your Google Mail, Yahoo! Mail, Hotmail and more. Microsoft Exchange users can also have their work emails sent straight to the device and we'll explain exactly how to do this in the Getting Connected chapter (*see* pages 94–151).

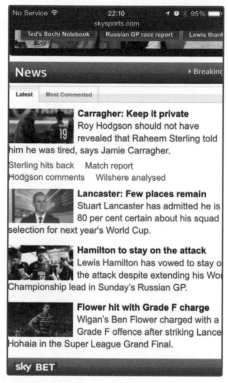

Above: iPhone's Safari browser allows you to access websites on the internet.

FaceTime

FaceTime is an Apple-to-Apple free video chat app which uses the front-facing camera. You can also make FaceTime Audio calls, meaning you can contact anyone using an iPhone, iPad or iPod touch (plus most newer Mac computers) for free using Wi-Fi or mobile data.

INTERNET

The iPhone is the entire internet in your pocket and can be accessed through apps or the built-in Safari browser.

App Store

Each icon on your iPhone's Home screen is an app (Mail, Phone, etc.), but there are thousands more of these self-contained applications in the App Store. They are a great way to keep your phone fresh with exciting new content.

Maps

The iPhone has a built-in Maps application made by Apple. It allows users to search for directions, but can also replace your sat nav unit with its voice-guided, turn-by-turn navigation feature.

MULTIMEDIA

The iPhone is also a full-on personal media player and games console packed into a pocket-size device. We'll be going into greater detail on all of these features throughout this guide.

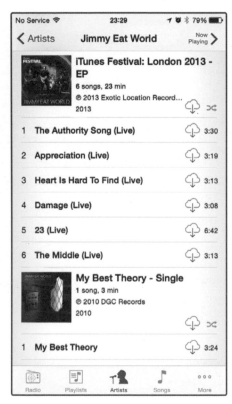

Above: The Music app is incorporated into the iPhone, allowing you to listen to music on the go.

Music

The first iPhone incorporated the revolutionary iPod music player, which allowed users to load their digital music collection on to the portable device. It's now known as the Music app. You can also buy music from the iTunes Store, or use music streaming apps in order to listen to tunes over the internet.

Video

As with music, you can also transfer your favourite digital movies and TV shows on to the iPhone for small-screen playback. The iTunes app offers the chance to buy or rent the latest movies and television shows while you're on the move.

Games

The iPhone has become a popular handheld gaming device thanks to addictive games like Candy Crush. Old favourites, such as Scrabble and Monopoly, are available to play too, while versions of console games can also be downloaded.

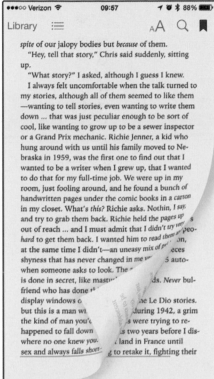

Above: The iBooks app allows you to access a bookstore through which millions of titles can be purchased, downloaded and read on your iPhone.

Hot Tip

Use the Photo Library portion of iCloud to save your photos online automatically.

Books

Apple offers an app and accompanying bookstore (iBooks – *see* page 207) that allows access to 2.5 million books, available to download and be read directly on the iPhone.

CAMERA

The camera on more recent iPhone models is so good that you can probably start leaving your trusty compact camera or camcorder at home on most occasions and not worry about precious memories being tinged by terrible photos.

Photography

The stills camera has got progressively better since it was an afterthought on the first iPhone (only 2 megapixels!). All iPhones since the iPhone 4S have 8-megapixel cameras, which have continued to improve all the way up to the iPhone 6 and 6 Plus.

Video Camera

The video camera on the iPhone allows users to record full high-definition video at 1080p (a resolution of 1920 x 1080), the same as most video cameras on the market and the same as television shows and movies you see in hi-def.

ANATOMY OF AN iPHONE

The new iPhone 6 and 6 Plus arguably represent the pinnacle of modern mobile technology. In this section, we'll explain some of the design intricacies, the features within the device itself, and the functions of the physical buttons and switches. But first, let's crack open the packaging.

WHAT'S IN THE BOX?

The first time you see that small box, you'd be forgiven for thinking: 'Is this what all the fuss is about?' However, within that minimalist packaging is everything you'll need to harness that new smartphone sitting invitingly within the box.

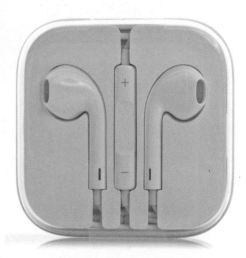

Above: The Apple EarPods headphones, with volume controls seen in the centre .

Earphones

Apple gives you a free pair of earphones with every iPhone for listening to media and hands-free calling. Apple calls them EarPods, as they're designed to fit the ear canal better, while also featuring a microphone and volume controls. Earlier versions of the iPhone earphones were much more basic.

Charger and Cable

With moderate use, the iPhone's battery should get you through the day, but it will need replenishing overnight. The charging cable slots into the mains adapter, while the other end slots into the bottom of the iPhone. The cable can also be plugged into the USB port on your computer in order to charge, sync or transfer content between the latter and your iPhone (see page 20). Apple launched a new, smaller Lightning cable with the iPhone 5.

iPHONE EXPLAINED: BUTTONS

Although most of your activities will be conducted via the touch screen (opening apps, typing, taking photos, playing music), the iPhone still has a few essential buttons and switches:

❶ Power Button

Holding down this button – positioned on the right-hand side of the iPhone 6 and 6 Plus and on the top of all older devices – for a second will allow you to switch your iPhone on and off. Pressing it once will wake the screen from its slumber.

Volume keys ❸

Mute switch ❹

Speakers ❼
Connector port ❻

Power button ❶

Headphone jack ❺
Home button ❷

❷ Home Button

Pressing the circular button in the centre will always bring you back to your Home screen. Pressing it when the device is asleep will wake up the screen; pressing it twice in quick succession will launch the multitasking bar, allowing you to switch between apps, whereas holding it down for a second will launch Siri (iPhone 4S and up). On the iPhone 5S, iPhone 6 and iPhone 6 Plus, the Home button also houses the Touch ID fingerprint sensor, which allows authorized users to unlock the phone without a passcode, authorize payments and more.

❸ Volume Keys

The two volume buttons are placed on the left side of the handset and allow you to adjust the volume of calls and media. In many cases, this can also be achieved by using a sliding bar on the touch screen.

> **Hot Tip**
>
> The volume buttons can also be used to trigger the camera (*see* page 17).

❹ Mute Switch

There are few things more embarrassing than your Star Wars ringtone blaring in the classroom, cinema or during an important meeting. You can quickly curtail 'The Imperial March' by flicking the Mute switch above the volume keys.

❺ Headphone Jack

The headphone jack sits on the bottom of the iPhone (in some much older versions, it was on top). You can use this to plug in the bundled-in earphones, your own set or any speaker that has a 3.5 mm connector cable.

❻ Connector Port

The connector at the bottom of the device allows you to charge your iPhone's battery, and to plug it into your computer to transfer content and synchronize important data (*see* image on the previous page). As explained previously in this chapter, Apple introduced a new connector with the iPhone 5.

❼ Speakers

There are two speakers on the iPhone 5: one in the earpiece, which allows you to hear calls, and another, more powerful one, on the bottom of the device, which plays ringtones, music and other audio (*see* image on page 19).

OTHER PHYSICAL CHARACTERISTICS

① Screen

The iPhone 5C and 5S models have a 4-inch screen; the iPhone 6 has a 4.7-inch screen; while the iPhone 6 Plus is 5.5 inches. Larger screens mean widescreen video and room for more apps.

Rear Camera ④

Flash

FaceTime Camera ③

Screen ①

Retina Display ②

② Retina Display

iPhones feature Apple's Retina Display technology, meaning photos, text and videos appear much clearer to the eye (these screens have more pixels than the human eye can distinguish when the phone is held at arm's length). The iPhone 6 Plus has the highest-res screen yet.

③ FaceTime Camera

On the iPhone 4, Apple introduced a front-facing camera, which enabled video calls over its FaceTime app (see page 15) but it can also be used for stills photography, like self-portraits.

④ Rear Camera

The back of an iPhone features a lens, which is much smaller than the one in a compact camera, and appears in the top-left corner of the device. There's also a flash sitting next to the lens.

Use Protection!

The iPhone isn't a cheap piece of kit to replace. To help keep it pristine, we'd suggest buying a case to safeguard it against drops, and a screen protector to guard against scratches and scuffs.

Hot Tip

The camera flash can also be used as a torch. Swipe up from the very bottom of the screen to access the Control Center and select the flashlight icon.

INSIDE YOUR iPHONE

The iPhone may look pretty, but it's on the inside that the magic is created. Each generation of iPhone has become progressively faster, more powerful and more versatile. Below is a list of some of the internal features.

- **Processor:** The iPhone 6 and 6 Plus feature the Apple A8 processor, which makes them the fastest, most powerful iPhones yet.

- **Storage:** The newest iPhone models now offer three storage options: 16 GB, 64 GB and 128 GB. The larger the capacity, the more music, video, apps and photos you can store on the device.

- **Battery:** Unlike some smartphones on the market, the iPhone's battery is not removable. If It dies, you'll need to take it to the Apple Store to be replaced.

- **Wi-Fi:** Providing you have the password, this allows you to connect to any wireless network and access internet-based content.

- **Mobile internet:** The iPhone has mobile data connectivity that allows you to access the 3G or 4G internet on the go. Your mobile network (O2, Vodafone, etc.) will place a limit on how much data you can use each month as part of your contract.

- **Bluetooth:** Via Bluetooth is one of the best ways of sharing photos or connecting to other devices. Use Bluetooth speakers to play music wirelessly on your iPhone. The newer iPhones contain Bluetooth 4.0 LE technology, which causes much less strain on the battery life.

- **GPS:** The chip inside your iPhone allows satellites to pinpoint your location and use mapping services.

- **NFC:** The iPhone 6 range has a built-in Near-Field Communications chip, which will be used to help iPhone users to pay for goods and services using their phone. The Apple Pay feature has no firm arrival date in the UK, so we won't discuss it within the book.

GETTING STARTED

Now we're familiar with the iPhone, both inside and out, it's almost time to push that Power button for the first time. In this section, we'll get you past all of the tedious pre-use steps and the boring, but necessary, setup screens.

Above: All iPhone models since 2012 require a nano-SIM, but older ones use a slightly larger micro-SIM.

THE SIM CARD

If this is your first iPhone, you'll almost certainly need a new SIM card. This card is embedded with a chip containing all your personal information and communicates with your mobile network. The iPhone 5, 5S, 5C, 6 and 6 Plus require a nano-SIM, the smallest yet.

Activating the New SIM Card

When you purchase your iPhone, you should be provided with a new SIM card. Your network should take care of transferring your current phone number and details over to the new SIM, allowing you to just insert-and-go. In some circumstances, it may be necessary to call the network to activate the new SIM. They may ask for the SIM card number and iPhone serial number. It's always better to do this before you attempt to activate your iPhone.

Hot Tip

If you insert the SIM and then receive an 'activation failed' message onscreen, you'll know it hasn't been activated yet. Call your network: it'll take minutes to fix.

Inserting the SIM Card

As with SIM activation (*see* left), if you have bought or intend to buy the iPhone in-store, then the staff there will be more than happy to help you through these steps:

1. Place the SIM tray eject tool (or you can use a bent paperclip) into the pinhole on the right side of the device.

2. Slowly withdraw the pin to release the SIM tray.

3. Remove the SIM card from its plastic housing and place the SIM card into the SIM tray so the chip faces down.

4. Carefully replace the SIM tray until it's firmly closed.

POWER UP

Out of the box, the iPhone arrives with a moderate amount of battery charge. Simply hold down the Power button on top of the phone for a second and you'll see the Apple logo, which stays in place for about 20 seconds.

SETTING UP YOUR iPHONE

Once the Apple logo disappears, you'll see a welcome screen. Swipe right where requested to enter the Set-Up Assistant and tap the touch screen to make selections. In the following pages there are some step-by-step guides to each of the screens you'll encounter.

Above: Use a paperclip or eject tool, as shown here, to release the SIM tray.

Above: When you first turn on your new iPhone, you will be greeted with the iPhone setup screen. Slide the arrow across and follow the instructions to set up your phone.

Above: Scroll down to select your country of residence and then press 'Next' in the top right-hand corner of the screen.

Above: You can select a Wi-Fi network and enter the password. This will then become the default source of internet whenever possible.

Language and Country

The first two screens ask you to select your language and country of residence. English is selected as default, so if that's your preference, touch the blue arrow in the top right of the screen to move forward. On the Country or Region screen, use a finger to scroll down to United Kingdom (or wherever) and repeat.

Choose a Wi-Fi Network

Next, the iPhone will ask you to configure a Wi-Fi network to assist with the setup. You can do this through your mobile internet data, but we'd recommend using Wi-Fi if possible.

1. After a few seconds, the screen will display available Wi-Fi networks and their respective signal strengths. Those which have a padlock icon next to the signal indicator mean that you'll need a password for access.

2. Touch the network of your choice. It'll either be named after a place (e.g. Starbucks, Home Network) or retain the codename written on the router (e.g. NETGEAR ZW52).

3. Enter the password, which will also be written on your Wi-Fi router, by typing it in using the onscreen virtual keyboard.

4. Press Join to move on to the next screen. If the password is incorrect, you'll be asked to enter it again.

Connect to iTunes (optional)

You can set up the iPhone 'over the air,' meaning that you don't have to connect to a computer any more. However, the 'Connect to a Wi-Fi network' screen still gives you the opportunity to 'Connect to iTunes' and continue the setup that way, as explained below.

1. Plug the provided charging cable into the bottom of the iPhone and plug the other end into the USB port of your desktop/laptop.

2. If you have it installed already, iTunes will launch. If you don't have it or need to update to a newer version, then go to www.apple.com/itunes and follow the download and installation instructions.

3. Your iPhone should now show up in the navigation bar within iTunes. Follow the onscreen instructions to complete the setup.

Above: Connect your iPhone to your laptop or desktop computer using the charging cable or via Wi-Fi in order to transfer music you may have stored in iTunes to your new iPhone.

Location Services

Next, you'll be asked whether you'd like to enable Location Services. This is important if you'd like to use the Maps app, or to use apps that rely on knowing your location. It can also be used to 'geo-tag' photos and social networking posts (e.g. when someone uses the 'Check In' feature on Facebook).

Set Up as New iPhone

From the Set Up iPhone screen, you should select the Set Up as New iPhone option and press Next. The other options are Restore from iCloud Backup and Restore from iTunes Backup. These are great options if you've owned an iPhone before or need to restore the device.

Apple ID

An Apple ID allows you to download apps, purchase media content, sync your accounts and much more. If you have an Apple ID, insert the username and password here. If not, you can easily set up a free account:

1. Insert your birthday as a means of retrieving your password.

2. Enter your name and email address (or set up an @icloud.com account there and then) and then choose a password.

3. Answer some security questions and remember them.

4. Select a 'rescue email address' if you wish (this will help if you forget your password) and opt in or out of Apple marketing emails. Agree to the Apple terms and conditions.

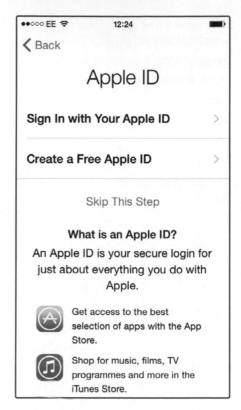

Above: Set up your Apple ID to start accessing the App Store, iCloud and iTunes.

iCloud

iCloud is Apple's free online storage and backup service. Its most basic function is to ensure that your contacts, documents, photos, mail and calendar are saved on servers in case your device is lost or stolen. It's great for remembering the apps, music, books and video you've purchased from iTunes and allowing you to re-download them at your convenience. You'll also be asked to upgrade iCloud Drive (iOS 8 only), which allows you to store more files and access them on other iOS devices or Mac computers (*see* Advanced iPhone, page 218).

Find My iPhone

Selecting Use Find My iPhone will allow you to track the geographical positioning of the device should you lose it. It'll also allow you to lock and wipe the device using iCloud.com, thus safeguarding all of your data. Accept this option: you have nothing to lose – except your iPhone.

Enable Messages and FaceTime

These enable free text, picture, voice and video communications with other iPhone/iPad/Mac users. Messages and FaceTime are two of the most-used features on iPhones.

Touch ID

If you own an iPhone 5S, iPhone 6 or iPhone 6 Plus, you'll be asked to set up the Touch ID fingerprint sensor. This adds an extra layer of security to your phone by requiring you to enter your print to open it. When prompted, place your finger or thumb on the sensor. You'll need to do this multiple times to capture the entire print. Once complete, Touch ID can be used to unlock the phone, confirm app purchases and more.

Passcode

You should also enter a four-digit passcode (mandatory if using Touch ID), which is needed to access your phone when locked. Don't make the passcode something too obvious, like your birth year.

Hot Tip

Apple-to-Apple messages are sent over the web and are not charged to your text message allowance. These 'iMessages' appear in blue within the text thread.

Above: Adding a fingerprint using Touch ID adds an extra layer of security to your iPhone.

iCloud Keychain

This is a new feature in iOS 8 and saves all of your passwords and personal data so it can be accessed across other Apple devices. Not a necessary step for new users.

Above: When setting up your iPhone, you will be asked if you want to enable Siri, which is a voice-controlled personal assistant.

Siri or No Siri?

The next setup screen asks whether you'd like to enable Siri: the voice-controlled personal assistant available on all newer iPhones (iPhone 4S and up).

> # Hot Tip
> If Siri has trouble understanding you, it may be your accent. Go to Settings > General > Siri > Language to select English (UK) instead of English (US).

Diagnostics

Here, you're asked if you want to send information to Apple about how you use your phone, so they can improve it.

Standard or Zoomed view

On the iPhone 6/6 Plus, you can choose between the standard and zoomed view. The latter offers larger icons and text, which may make the device more accessible for users with visual impairments.

Setup Complete

The final screen thanks you for setting up your iPhone. Selecting Start using iPhone will take you to the Home screen. There's so much more still to set up, such as your email and social networks, but these will be tackled later in the book. For now, let's explore your new iPhone.

iPHONE BASICS

Over the course of the next few pages, we'll offer some basic tips on familiarizing yourself with the Home screen, moving around the device, using the touch screen, typing on the keyboard and more.

THE iPHONE

The screenshot on the right illustrates the iPhone 6's Home screen after you've first set up the device; below are some of the key elements to take note of.

1 iPhone Title Bar

The iPhone title bar features many vital indicators, described here from left to right.

2 Signal strength: The more bars you see, the stronger your mobile signal. This affects your ability to make clear voice calls and send texts.

3 Network identity: Here, you'll see the name of the network you're registered to (O2, Vodafone, Three, etc.).

4 Internet: If you're connected to Wi-Fi, you'll see the fan icon. Once again, the fullness of the fan represents the strength of the signal. If you're using mobile internet, you'll usually see the letters 3G or LTE. If there's zero connectivity, you'll see a small circle.

Above: The iPhone 6's Home screen.

Hot Tip
To view battery life as a percentage in the title bar, hit Settings > General > Usage > Battery Usage and toggle the Battery Percentage switch to 'On'.

Location/
Compass arrow   Clock   Bluetooth
③   ②   ①

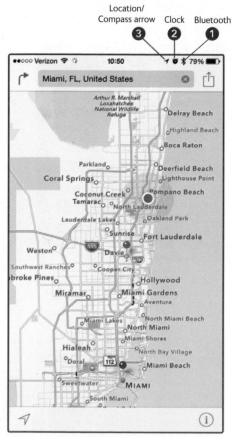

Above: Maps screen with compass arrow.

⑤ **Time:** Displays the current time.

⑥ **Battery:** The battery icon shows, proportionately, how much battery you've used. Once you get to 20 per cent or lower, it will turn red.

Other Title Bar Indicators

Here are some further indicators that may occasionally appear within the title bar, depending on what's running on the iPhone:

① **Bluetooth**: This will only appear when using Bluetooth (see page 69). The Bluetooth icon is a B infused with an antenna.

② **Clock**: If you've set an alarm, a stopwatch or a timer, a clock icon will be present.

③ **Location**: If you're using Maps or your iPhone is scanning for your location, the compass arrow will appear in the title bar.

Play: If music or video is playing, a play icon will appear.

Airplane: If you have enabled Airplane Mode, which disables all mobile and wireless functionality while still allowing you to use other features when flying, a plane icon will appear in place of the mobile signal bars.

Compass arrow: Will let you know if location-based apps are in use.

APP ICONS

Most of your iPhone's Home screen is taken up by rows of apps.

Hot Tip

If there's a red circle with a number next to an app icon, it means you've received a notification. It could be an email, message, missed call or news of an app update.

Below: You can have multiple home screens and also place like-minded applications into folders.

Dock

This is at the foot of the Home screen and maintains the same four icons at all times. The idea is to include the apps that you use most, in order to make them more accessible. The apps that appear by default are Phone, Mail, Safari and Music.

App Folders

Like-minded apps like Notes and Reminders can be placed in Folders under names like Utilities. This makes the phone easier to navigate. Drag one app on to another to create a new folder, and give it a name.

Multiple Home Screens

The iPhone arrives with two screens of apps, but when they're full, more will open up. In order to move between them, swipe a finger left or right across the touch screen. The white dots beneath the bottom row of apps indicate which screen you are currently on.

Spotlight Search Screen

Dragging your finger in a downward motion on the touch screen reveals a search field. Type here to quickly find a contact, an app, an email, a calendar event, an app store listing or a Wikipedia page.

BASIC iPHONE NAVIGATION

It's time to learn a few of the basic touch-screen gestures.

Opening Applications

Each of the four-sided icons on your Home screen is an application. Simply touching one of these icons will open that app, full screen, on your iPhone.

Above: The multitasking screen also features access to your recently used contacts.

Going Home

Whatever you're doing with your iPhone, pressing the physical iPhone button will take you right back to the Home screen.

Summon Siri

You can bring up the iPhone's personal voice assistant by holding down the Home button for a couple of seconds. The phone will make a unique sound to denote the launch and a microphone will appear at the foot of the screen. Press the microphone icon to begin using Siri (*see p.227* for more on how to harness Siri).

Multitasking

iOS features a multitasking tool, allowing you to move between apps without returning to the Home screen. Double-click the Home button to reveal cards showing the apps you currently have open. Swipe left and right to find your app of choice and tap the card to re-open it.

Swiping

Moving your finger across the page to move to the next screen is a key means of navigating your way around the iPhone and will become second nature.

Scrolling

If you're reading a web page, email, a thread of text messages or moving around an app and wish to move up and down the page, use a finger to flick the screen up or down. The faster the flick, the faster the page moves.

Zooming

The iPhone enables many multi-touch gestures; the most popular of these is zooming.

- **To zoom in**: Place your thumb and forefinger on the screen and move them both away from each other.

- **To zoom out**: Place your thumb and forefinger on the screen and move them towards each other in a pinching motion.

Left & above: Videos can be viewed in portrait (left) and landscape (above).

Accelerometer

The iPhone has a built-in sensor that knows when you switch the view from portrait to landscape – essentially turning the handset on its side. This is called an accelerometer. It works well with apps that require typing, as it increases the size of the keyboard, and with the Camera Roll app while viewing pictures and videos. Some websites also have greater readability in landscape.

Above: Turning the phone to landscape increases the size of the messaging keyboard.

The iPhone Keyboard

The iPhone's virtual keyboard has a QWERTY layout. Here are the other basic keyboard buttons.

○ **Shift:** Press the upward arrow once to type a single capital letter. Hit it twice in quick succession and it'll turn lighter grey and turn on the Caps Lock.

Above: The iOS 8 keyboard.

○ **123:** This button switches the keyboard from letters to numbers and symbols.

○ **Globe:** Tapping this will allow you to add a range of 'emoji'-like smiley faces to your messages.

○ **Microphone:** Dictate the message to your iPhone, rather than typing it.

○ **Space:** Just like the space bar on your computer, this allows you to move from one word to the next.

○ **Return:** Create a new line on which to type.

○ **Delete:** Touching the cross enables you to delete any entered text. Pressing it once will delete a letter, whereas holding it down will delete at a faster rate.

Lock the Screen/iPhone

If you're not using the iPhone, pressing the power button once will turn off the screen and lock the phone; if you're playing music, this will not affect playback.

Waking the iPhone

If you've locked the screen or it has timed out due to inactivity (see Auto-Lock on page 41), you can wake it by pressing the power button once and using the Slide to unlock functionality.

If you've chosen a security passcode (*see* page 29), you'll be asked to enter this. If you've enabled Touch ID, place your digit on the sensor to unlock the phone. The iPhone will then return to the screen you were viewing when the device was locked.

iPhone Lock Screen

There's plenty you can achieve from the lock screen:

- **Media Control Panel:** When playing music, double-click the Home button to summon a media control panel to pause, skip or adjust the volume.

- **Summon Siri:** Hold down the Home button to summon Siri.

- **Camera app:** Drag the camera icon into the centre of the screen to launch the Camera app without unlocking the phone.

- **Alerts:** If you receive a message/email/notification, simply swipe the notification to go straight to it, after using your Passcode or Touch ID.

- **Control/Notifications Centers:** Access Control Center and Notifications Center by swiping up or down from the top or bottom of the screen respectively.

Above: Media controls, the camera app and Siri can still be used from the iPhones lock screen.

Shut Down

In order to switch off the iPhone, simply hold down the power switch for around 2–3 seconds when the phone is unlocked. The screen will go dark aside from a swipe bar, which requires you to 'slide to power off'. You can touch the cancel bar to return to the Home screen.

BASIC iPHONE SETTINGS

Without getting too deep into the nitty gritty at this stage, here are a few basic settings that you may wish to adjust while using your iPhone. In order to access them, press the grey Settings icon on the Home screen.

Below: The Control Center offers quick access to key settings by swiping up from the bottom of the screen.

CONTROL CENTER

The iOS Settings app is home to the nuts and bolts of the OS, but you can quickly adjust some settings from the Control Center. Simply swipe directly up from the bottom of the screen to bring up the menu. Here are the settings you can quickly toggle:

○ **Airplane Mode:** Switches off all cellular and internet activity. Perfect when flying or in a meeting.

○ **Wi-Fi:** Turn Wi-Fi on and off.

○ **Bluetooth:** Turn this connectivity tool on and off.

○ **Do Not Disturb:** Represented by the moon icon. DND settings can be adjusted in the main settings app.

○ **Portrait Orientation Lock:** Touching this icon prevents the phone switching to landscape when turned on its side.

○ **Screen Brightness:** Slide the meter left or right to alter this setting.

- **Music:** These controls are handy when playing tunes, allowing you to play, stop, skip or alter volume.

- **AirDrop:** A tool for sharing files with other Apple users.

- **Airplay:** Allows you to send media to AirPlay-enabled devices like Apple TV over Wi-Fi.

- **Torch:** Switch your device's flashlight (the camera flash) on and off.

- **Timer, Calculator and Camera:** Tapping these icons takes you straight to these apps.

BRIGHTNESS

As well as doing so from the Control Center, you can change this setting by selecting Settings > Display & Brightness in iOS 8 (Brightness & Wallpaper in iOS 7). Touching the blue brightness bar and dragging it left or right will decrease or increase brightness.

WALLPAPER

By selecting Settings > Wallpaper (Brightness & Wallpaper in iOS 7) you can also alter the appearance of your phone. On the left is the lock screen wallpaper and on the right is the Home screen wallpaper. Select Choose a New Wallpaper to change them to a new wallpaper or to a photo from your Camera Roll. Once you've chosen the new picture, press Set.

Hot Tip

While optimal screen brightness is preferable, it also has a negative effect on battery life, which can be preserved by turning the brightness down.

Below: Newer versions of iOS offer Dynamic wallpapers, which look like they move, but these cause greater drain on battery life.

SOUNDS

You can tinker with the sounds emanating from your phone when calls or notifications arrive.

Changing Ringtones and App Alerts

Enter Settings > Sounds to control volume and vibration, and to customize sounds for each volume type. The Sounds and Vibration Patterns menu allows you to control the precise sound and vibration style for each type of notification. For example, press Text Tone to bring up all of the available options. Selecting one of the options will place a tick next to the name and play a preview. Once you're happy with your choice, press the Back button and your selection will be saved.

Below: You can increase the security of your iPhone by choosing a passcode. You will need to enter the passcode each time you unlock your phone.

Controlling Ringer Volume

To adjust your ringtone volume, simply drag the onscreen slider left or right within the Settings > Sounds menu. It's also easy to control the ringtone volume by pressing the physical volume keys on the side of the device when on the Home screen. This will bring up an onscreen indicator showing the volume meter increasing or decreasing.

SECURITY

Losing a smartphone can be more dangerous than losing your credit cards, bank details and address book in one fell swoop. Here's how to protect your data.

Passcode and Touch ID

When we set up the iPhone, we added a four-digit Passcode and a Touch ID fingerprint. Both prevent unwanted guests accessing your iPhone beyond the lock screen. If you skipped this step on setup, enter Settings and select General. Scroll down to Touch ID and Passcode. You'll then go through the steps listed earlier in this chapter to shore up your defences.

Auto-Lock

Within Settings > General > Auto-Lock you can configure the period of inactivity necessary for the phone to lock itself. The default is 1 minute, but you can choose from between Never and 5 minutes.

SYNCING CONTENT ON YOUR iPHONE

There are a number of ways to ensure that the information you carry around with you on your iPhone is up to date. You can sync information using iTunes and iCloud; both have their merits and we'd advise you make use of both.

Syncing iTunes via USB

The traditional way to sync content on an iPhone is to plug it into your computer via the bundled-in USB cable. Once you plug the device in, the iTunes program should launch (*see* Downloading iTunes on page 187). You'll see your iPhone appear as a button in the navigation bar in iTunes (the latest version is iTunes 12). Click the iPhone icon and select the Sync option at the bottom of the Summary tab.

Syncing via iTunes over Wi-Fi

With newer versions of iOS (iOS 5 and higher) and iTunes (v10.5 and above) loaded, you can sync content over Wi-Fi when both your computer and iPhone are on the same Wi-Fi network. Here's how to set it up:

1. Plug the iPhone into your computer; iTunes will launch. Select your iPhone from the top navigation menu. In the Summary tab, scroll down to the Options section.

Hot Tip

Selecting 'Never' from the Auto-Lock settings screen will mean your screen will stay on unless you manually hit the power button. This will drain your battery life fast.

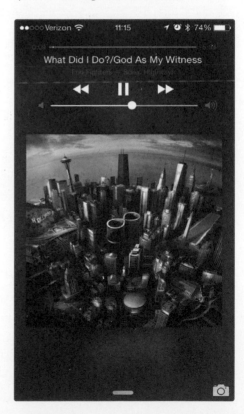

Below: To keep your iPhone up to date, you can sync it to iTunes using Wi-Fi or a USB cable.

2. Tick the box which says 'Sync with this iPhone over Wi-Fi' and press Sync to save the changes.

3. iTunes syncing will now take place when your phone and computer are on the same network.

What Information is Synced via iTunes?

iTunes syncs all of the applications, music, TV shows, movies, web bookmarks, books, contacts, calendars, notes, documents and ringtones you have downloaded. iTunes will also download new content you've acquired via your phone and vice versa, ensuring a consistent experience across your phone and computer.

Syncing Your iPhone via iCloud

If you agreed to use iCloud when setting up the device, it will automatically sync information from some of the iPhone's most important applications, making that information seamlessly available at iCloud.com and across any other Apple devices you may have.

What is Synced via iCloud?

Enter Settings > iCloud to choose what information you'd like to sync to your iCloud account. Among the options are: Contacts, Calendars, Reminders, Safari (and bookmarks), Notes, Photo Stream and more. Turning these on in the iCloud settings will mean any changes you make are saved via iCloud.

Hot Tip

Syncing information via iCloud will not back up the information. If you delete a contact on your iPhone, it will be deleted from iCloud too.

Above: You can choose which aspects of your iPhone you wish to sync via iCloud.

BACKING UP YOUR iPHONE

A backup will restore your most important information if you need to perform a full reset or if you buy a new one and wish to pick up where you left off on a new device. You can choose to back up via iTunes or iCloud.

Backing Up via iCloud

Apple gives you 5 GB of free storage to store important data in the event you have to perform a full reset. If you choose to enable backups, press Settings > iCloud. Scroll down to Backup and toggle the switch to 'on'. If enabled, iCloud backups are automatically made when your phone is on a Wi-Fi network, plugged in and locked.

Backing Up via iTunes

The default setting is to back up via iCloud, but if you prefer to have everything physically backed up on your computer, you can do so via iTunes. Plug your phone into your computer and iTunes should load.

Above: Backing up using iCloud.

1. Select the iPhone in the iTunes menu.

2. From the Backup menu, tick the box that says Back up to this computer.

3. Select Apply to save the changes, and then press Sync to back up the phone. This will switch off the iCloud backup.

What Information is Backed Up?

Backups over iCloud and iTunes will safeguard all photos on your Camera Roll, all of your account settings (email, Facebook, Twitter, etc.), documents, general phone settings (wallpaper, ringtones, etc.), Contacts, Calendar and more, and make it easy to pick up where you left off if you restore from a backup.

iTunes vs iCloud: Which Should I Use?

As there are two options for backing up your data, it's sometimes difficult to pick the best one for you. Both options have their advantages; the following guide should help you decide.

- ● **iTunes:** If you prefer to have information saved on your computer rather than on the internet, choose iTunes. This can be the better option for restoring absolutely everything on your phone. Restoring an iPhone via USB connection is also faster than via iCloud.

- ● **iCloud:** To go truly wireless, you need to use iCloud. This will enable you to restore your device or set up a new phone with all of your information without connecting to a computer. Also, if you're not backing up that much data, Wi-Fi iCloud backups are quick and simple.

iOS SOFTWARE UPDATE

Apple releases a new version of iOS every year. The latest version is iOS 8, which came out in September 2014. It's not just the new iPhone 6 and 6 Plus that get iOS 8. If you own an iPhone 4S (released in 2011), you can also update and access the new features.

Updating Software

Once a new update is available, you'll receive a notification telling you it is ready to download. You'll also see a badge icon next to the Settings app. Go to Settings > General > Software Update to see what the update is. Here's how to download it:

> **Hot Tip**
>
> For everything you need to know about restoring from an iTunes or iCloud backup, see the Advanced iPhone chapter.

1. Back up your iPhone, in case something goes wrong. Ensure you're connected to Wi-Fi and your battery is at least half charged or connected to a power source.

2. Go to Settings > General > Software Update > Install Now.

3. The update should install (you'll see the progress meter).

4. Once complete, the iPhone will restart and you'll have the latest version of the software.

NOTIFICATIONS

The well-connected iPhone user is constantly receiving new information, emails, messages, social networking updates, upcoming Calendar events, Reminders, app updates, missed phone calls and more.

NOTIFICATION CENTER

To reveal the Notification Center, place your finger on or just above the title bar and drag it downward. There's a 'Today' section featuring calendar appointments, alarm clock settings, weather and upcoming birthdays. Tapping 'Notifications' shows all alerts from apps enabled in the Notifications settings. See page 46 for more on notifications.

Hot Tip

In order to remove an item from the Notification Center, touch the small cross on the right side of the message. This won't delete the message, just the notification.

Configuring the Notification Center

Enter Settings > Notifications to control which applications appear in the Notification Center. For example, if you don't want Mail notifications to appear, then select this from the list and toggle the Notification

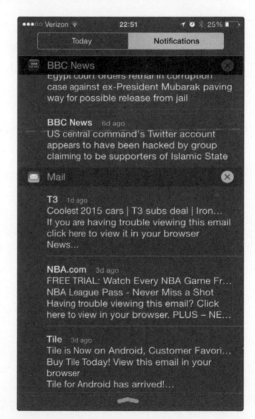

Above: The Notification Center is now a staple in iOS. It can be accessed by placing your finger on the title bar and dragging it downwards.

Center switch from 'on' to 'off'. Likewise, apps that aren't currently configured for Notification Center can be enabled using this method.

Alert Style

Within the Settings > Notifications menu you can also configure the type of alert you'll receive for each app. Select an app from the list and you'll see Alert Style.

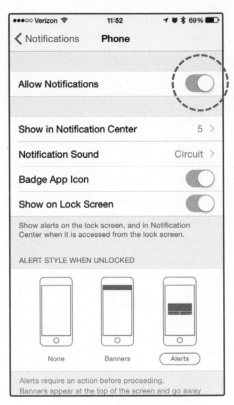

○ **None**: If you don't want to be alerted by this app then select None. This way, you'll only see updates from, for example, Facebook, if you manually enter the app.

○ **Banners**: A Banner notification appears at the top of the screen and then disappears automatically.

○ **Alerts**: Alerts appear in the center of the screen and require you to press Launch/Reply (to bring up the app) or Close (to deal with it later). These can be quite intrusive in apps like Messages, where you may be having a conversation, but great for ensuring you see important emails.

Above: You can choose how you would like an alert to appear on your screen.

○ **Notification Sound**: You can toggle this switch to choose which sound (if any) the app will make when an alert is received.

○ **Show on Lock Screen**: Selecting this option will ensure that a notification will be visible on the Lock screen.

ORGANIZING

Have we already mentioned that the iPhone is multi-talented? The device features a host of built-in apps to ensure you never sleep in, never burn dinner and always remember that Eureka idea.

CALENDAR

The iPhone's built-in Calendar app will sync all appointments from your email and social networking accounts (e.g. Facebook Events), while new events can be segregated into Work, School and Home sections. Apple's online storage iCloud platform ensures that any new appointments you add using your iPhone will appear across your other Apple devices.

Below: You can add specific events to your iPhone calendar and request multiple reminders.

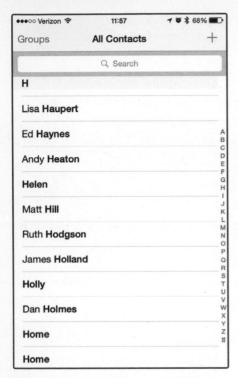

Above: The Contacts app allows you to scroll through your address book and select people to message or call.

ADDRESS BOOK

Your phone contacts should naturally be imported on to the device when you first insert the SIM card, but it's best to check with your network, as in some cases, you may have to back them up first. You can also import contacts from Microsoft Exchange, Facebook, Twitter, Google, iCloud and more. Learn how to manage your contacts in chapter two.

CALCULATOR

The built-in touch-screen calculator, which sits within the Utilities folder on your Home screen, makes it easy to split dinner bills, work out household budgets and even resolve complex formulas.

Hot Tip

Turn the iPhone on its side to switch to the scientific calculator.

CLOCK

As well as the clock that sits within the centre of your title bar, there is a standalone Clock app on your Home screen, which includes a World Clock, Alarm, Stopwatch and Timer.

World Clock

The World Clock is a handy feature. By default, the iPhone features Cupertino (Apple's headquarters in California), New York and London, but you can add other locations to the list.

Left: World Clock lets you view the time across multiple locations.

Alarm Clock

Mobile phones have been consigning the trusty alarm clock to the scrapheap for years, and the iPhone continues that tradition.

1. Select the Clock app, and press the Alarm icon at the bottom of the screen and press the + icon in the top right to add a new alarm.

2. Use the scrollable wheels to set the hour, minute and AM/PM settings. Press the Repeat option to select which days you'd like the alarm to go off.

3. Select Sound to choose an alarm (choose from default ringtones, a song from your music library or select 'Buy More Tones' to head to the iTunes store).

4. Toggle Snooze on or off to give you the option of an extra 10 minutes, and press Label to give the alarm a name, i.e. work, feed dog, etc. When you are satisfied, click Save to return to the Alarm screen. From there, you can toggle the alarm on or off.

5. Selecting the Edit button in the top-right corner enables you to delete the alarm completely or change the settings discussed above.

Stopwatch

Although now an afterthought on a smartphone, the stopwatch is still useful.

Hot Tip

You can exit the Clock app and the timer, stopwatch and alarm will continue to run in the background.

Above: Alarm Clock allows you to save multiple alarms with your choice of repeat, sound and snooze options.

Above: The timer screen gives you access to sound options as well as displaying cancel and pause buttons.

Hot Tip

You can set multiple alarms and choose the days that they will go off. For example, you can set an alarm to only go off on weekdays.

Timer

The Timer is the final option within the clock app.

1. Select Clock > Timer and use the vertical scroll wheels to set how many hours and how many minutes you'd like to count down from.

2. Choose an alert to sound when the timer runs out by selecting 'When Timer Ends' and choosing from available ringtones.

3. Press Start to begin the timer, and a new screen will launch, informing you of how long is left and also enabling you to pause or cancel the timer.

NOTES, REMINDERS AND VOICE MEMOS

The iPhone features a number of ways for you to preserve information you're liable to forget. In some cases, it will even send you endless reminders. Here are three apps that specialize in remembering, so you don't have to.

Notes

The built-in Notes app is given its own icon on the Home screen. All of your previous notes will be listed, accessible and editable with one touch. You can also select the on screen 'New' button to start a new note and use the keyboard to begin typing away. All notes will be automatically stored without having to save them.

Reminders

This excellent to-do list application allows you to check off items and receive alerts for things you haven't done yet. Various versions of the app operate differently, but here is how it works in iOS 8:

1. Launch Reminders in iOS 8 and you'll see a notebook-style layout. Click the + next to New List. This will summon the keyboard, allowing you to name the list. Press Done.

2. Enter the list and begin typing items on the notepad.

3. If this is the only item, then press Done, but if there's more, simply hit return on the keyboard to add a new one.

Hot Tip

To sync all of your notes to iCloud, hit Settings > iCloud and toggle the Notes switch to on. You can also change the font by entering Settings > Notes.

Above: Using the keyboard, the Notes app allows you to store thoughts, ideas and lists.

4. When you've completed the task, return to the app and tick the box next to the item. This will move the task to the Completed screen, which can be viewed by clicking the list icon in the top-left corner of the app.

5. In order to set reminders for future dates, touch the 'i' icon next to the list item. Here, you can select Remind me on a day or Remind me at a location.

6. Once completed, select Done to save your changes.

Geo-reminders

Reminders are really cool – you can even select Remind me at a location. For example, if you always forget to buy toothpaste, you can ask the iPhone to send you a notification when your GPS sensor detects that you're near the supermarket on a map. In order to achieve this, set the Reminder as explained above and then select the particular item to bring up the Details screen. Select Remind me at a location to enter an address and then you can choose to be reminded when you arrive at or leave that location.

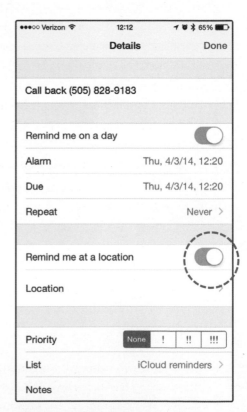

Above: You can choose to receive reminders when at a particular location.

> ## Hot Tip
> When setting geo-reminders, you can alter how near or far you are away before you get the notification by expanding the circle around your chosen location.

Voice Memos

The Voice Memos app allows you to record conversations, random great ideas, interviews, humorous anecdotes, messages for friends and family, and more.

1. Launch the Voice Memos app from within the Utilities folder on the Home screen.

2. Select the red record button to begin recording. A red 'Recording' bar will appear in the title bar, indicating the ongoing length of the recording.

3. The VU indicator will monitor the volume of the sound. It's best to keep it out of the red zone to ensure that the audio retains clarity.

4. If you wish to pause your recording at any point, hit the stop button (and again to restart). Once you've finished recording, press the Done button to the right. Name the voice recording and press save.

5. All recordings can be accessed using the 'list' button in the bottom right corner. Playback can be controlled from this screen.

You can exit the Voice Memo app while recording and use other phone functions without interrupting the recording. Just tap the red indicator on the title bar to return to the app.

Above: The VU indicator in the Voice Memos app allows you to keep track of recording volume.

USING THE iPHONE

MAKING CALLS

Despite being a multi-purpose tool, the iPhone is still a phone, used for making phone calls. Basic calling is simple: tap a name in your Contacts, tell Siri to 'call Chris', or touch a name to return a recent call – but there's much more. The iPhone also supports video and conference calls, and this section will show you how.

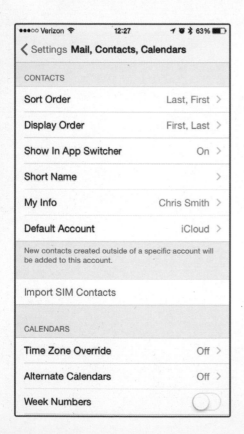

CONTACTS

Whether you are choosing who to share photos with or when to accept calls from colleagues, setting up your contacts in a smart way is crucial for making your iPhone work harder for you.

There are numerous ways to add contacts: from importing from a SIM card to syncing using iTunes. Once imported (*see* below), you'll find phone numbers, email addresses, Twitter and Facebook info for everyone in your address book. Tap the Phone app, press the Contacts icon, and from there you can apply some simple iOS 8 magic to really make your phonebook work for you.

Importing Contacts

How you add your old contacts on to your new iPhone will depend on where they are stored. The most common ways to achieve this are the following:

Left: You can import contacts from a SIM card. This is the best way to transfer such information across from your old phone to your new iPhone.

○ **From a SIM card**: Insert the SIM card containing all your contacts into your new iPhone (but remember that iPhone 5 and up require a smaller nano-SIM, so if yours are stored on a regular SIM card, you'll need to choose an alternative option). Go to Settings > Mail, Contacts, Calendars > Import SIM Contacts.

○ **Switching from Google Android?** You can back up your contacts to your Google account on your old phone. Then go to Settings > Mail, Contacts, Calendars. Add your Google account and you'll then be given the option to import your contacts.

○ **From iTunes**: Copying contacts from an old iPhone? Simply make an iTunes backup of the old phone (*see* page 43). Connect your old phone to iTunes via a USB cable, then right-click on your device in iTunes and select Backup. After that's complete, connect your new iPhone via USB, right-click on it in iTunes and select Restore from Backup.

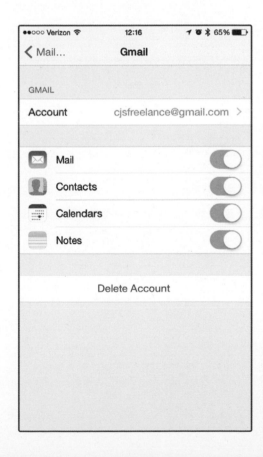

○ **From iCloud**: If your old iPhone was running iOS 5 or iOS 6 you can sync your contacts using iCloud. On the old device, go to Settings > iCloud > Storage & Backup and make sure that iCloud is switched on. Then do the same on your new device.

○ **From a Microsoft Exchange Global Address List**: Go to Settings > Mail, Contacts, Calendars, select your Exchange account and turn on Contacts.

Right: You can transfer your contacts from a Google Android phone by backing them up to Gmail and then importing contacts when you add a Google account.

Importing Contacts from Facebook

iPhone users who want to connect their Facebook contacts with their iPhone address book now have a super-fast way to do just that. Before you do this, though, it's worth deciding whether having all your Facebook friends in your Contacts is desirable. In most cases, you'll need to link Facebook entries manually with the contacts already in your iPhone which, depending on how active you are, could be hundreds and clutter up your Contacts.

1. Activate your Facebook account on your iPhone: open Settings, select Facebook and enter your Facebook account details. In iOS 8, this will automatically download your Facebook friends' information to the Contacts app.

2. Your Facebook friends' details will automatically be integrated, where available, and a Group called Facebook will be created in your Contacts.

3. Tap Update Contacts at any time in Settings > Facebook to ensure the information remains up to date. This will match email addresses in your Contacts to your Facebook friends and match them up.

Importing Contacts from Twitter

It's also possible to add your Twitter contacts into your Contacts. Once again, be aware that this could mean hundreds of people, depending on how active you are, and you'll need to merge Twitter entries with people already in your iPhone manually.

Left: By activating your Facebook account on your phone, you can integrate 'friends' into your contact list.

1. Activate your Twitter account on your iPhone: open Settings, select Twitter and enter your Twitter account details.

2. After connecting with Twitter, click Update Contacts. This will place the Twitter contacts into your Contacts. You'll usually find them under their full name (or what they told Twitter their full name was).

Merging Duplicate Contacts

You can merge duplicate contacts, from SIM, iCloud, Facebook and Twitter, into one entry in your Contacts app. Open the contact in question, click Edit in the top-right corner of the page for that entry and then scroll down to the bottom to find the Link Contact button. Tap this and select the contact(s) you wish to link.

Adding Contacts Manually

There are two main methods for adding new people into your Contacts:

○ **Brand new contact**: From within Contacts, tap the + button. This will bring up a form for you to fill in with the person's details, such as First Name, Last Name, Phone Number, Email and Address. From here, you can also assign things such as ringtone, text tone and photo, or apply social networking preferences.

○ **Previous caller**: Open your Recent Call list and scroll to the number you wish to add. Tap on the blue arrow next to it and then select 'Create New Contact'. You can then enter the relevant information.

Below: You can add and edit contacts manually, and can choose to include extra details such as an address.

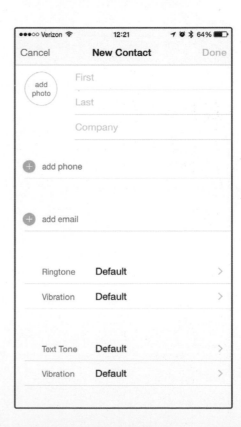

SYNCING CONTACTS

Once you have imported your contacts on to your iPhone, you need to ensure they're kept safe and up to date. It's now easier than ever to back up and synchronize vital information, and to make it readily available to access wherever you are and across all your devices – computer, iPad, iPod or other iPhone. For those desperate to go wireless, Apple's new iCloud feature also lets you sync your iPhone contacts and data over the air, without having to plug the device into a computer, but we'll also explain the traditional method of using iTunes and cables.

Below: While connected to Wi-Fi, you can sync your contacts using iCloud by selecting 'iCloud' from the 'Settings' menu.

Choose Your Sync Weapon

Both iCloud and iTunes sync have their pros and cons, but it's important to choose one as your standard syncing option. If you alternate, or even do both simultaneously, you may end up with a phonebook full of duplicate data and cleaning up that won't be fun.

Syncing Contacts Using iCloud

Apple's web-based iCloud service now offers computer-free updates for your contacts and data, but you'll need to be connected to Wi-Fi before you follow these steps:

1. Tap Settings on your Home screen and choose iCloud.

2. Tap Account and, if you haven't already done so while setting up, add in your Apple ID and password.

3. From here, you can choose which of the services you'd like to sync using the On/Off switches. In this instance, you just need to ensure you've turned on Contacts.

Syncing Contacts Using iTunes

We wouldn't recommend this, but if you prefer to manage your information on a larger screen, then connecting to iTunes via a USB cable or over the same Wi-Fi network is your best bet, but first you'll have to turn off over-the-air syncing on iCloud.

1. Go to Settings > Mail, Contacts, Calendars, select iCloud and switch off Contacts.

2. Connect the iPhone to your computer and iTunes should launch automatically. If it doesn't, you'll need to open it manually by clicking on the icon on your computer desktop. If it is on the same Wi-Fi network, it should sync automatically.

3. Once iTunes is open, select your iPhone from the source list within iTunes.

4. Click the Info tab and find Sync contacts. Here, you can choose to synchronize all your contacts or identify selected Groups you wish to sync by ticking the boxes next to them.

Searching Contacts

Using the iPhone's tactile touch screen to scroll rapidly up and down through your Contacts list is probably the most intuitive way to find that person you want to call or email, but there are other shortcuts.

Hot Tip

If you want iTunes to launch and sync your iPhone automatically whenever you connect it to your computer, select the Summary tab and tick the box in the Options section that says 'Open iTunes when this iPhone is connected'.

Below: You can search your contacts by typing the name you are looking for into the search bar at the top of the screen. This will quickly filter through your contact list.

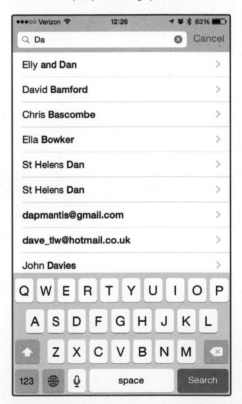

○ **Jump to contacts by letter**: Use the alphabet on the right to quickly view all the names on your list.

○ **Simple search**: Start typing the name of the contact you're hunting for into the search bar at the top of the screen. Your contacts will automatically filter to display matches.

Organizing Your Contacts Using Groups

Depending on which accounts you have added to your iPhone, contacts will be split into various Groups in your contact book. For example, Facebook, iCloud, Google and Twitter all get their own Groups. However, you can filter which Groups appear in your overall contacts listing – and here's how:

1. Enter Contacts and select Groups. At first, you're likely to see all Groups listed with a tick mark.

2. To turn off certain Groups (such as Facebook), you can tap a Group to remove the tick mark.

3. Tap Done and all the contacts within the Groups you selected will not show up.

Hot Tip

By default, the iPhone sorts contacts by last name, but often, you only have a first name. To order your contacts by first name go into Settings > Mail, Contacts, Calendar, toggle the Sort Order and switch to 'First, Last'.

••••○○ Verizon 🛜	12:30	✈ 🔆 ✲ 62% 🔋
Cancel		Done

edit

Chris

Smith

Chris

~~132 S Cypress Road~~

⊖ home > ~~(856) 471-6825~~

⊕ add phone

⊖ home > ~~christopheredworld@yog...~~

⊕ add email

| Ringtone | Default | > |
| Vibration | Default | > |

Above: Setting up a My Info card makes it easier to share all of your information in one fell swoop.

Editing and Deleting Contacts

In order to change contact information or delete someone who is now out of your good books, go to Contacts and select the entry you want to amend or remove. Once the contact is open, click Edit and you can freely add, amend and delete details using the green + buttons or the red circles. If you want to delete the contact entirely then scroll to the bottom and hit Delete Contact.

Sharing Contacts

'Can you send me their number?' is a question that gets most people scrabbling through their phonebook, before reading out the answer while someone else taps it into their phone; however, there is a faster way to share contacts. Simply tap the contact you wish to send, tap Share Contact and you can send the info by email, text message or AirDrop (see page 224).

SETTING UP YOUR 'MY INFO' CARD

The information on your 'My Info' card gets shared whenever you send someone your contact details. In order to edit this information, go to Settings > Mail, Contacts, Calendars and press My Info, then select your Contact Card. From here, you can add, edit and delete information and also adjust how Siri and other apps use your info.

FAVORITES

In iPhone speak, your Favorites are the numbers you call the most. Just like speed dial on a normal phone, you can store all the vital numbers you'll be dialling regularly for easy access and fewer taps, thus saving time when you want to call.

Adding Favorites

It'd be amazing if the iPhone could automatically fill up your Favorites group based on the number of times you've called people in your phonebook but, currently, anointing a Favorite is still your choice ... Plus, it might be embarrassing to have that takeaway listed at No. 1. There are two methods for adding a new Favorite:

- ○ **When you're viewing a contact**: An Add to Favorites button will appear on the screen. Tapping this brings up all of the phone numbers you have stored for that person. You can then select which number to make your Favorite for that contact.

- ○ **From within your Favorites**: Tap the + symbol in the top-right corner. This brings up your Contacts list where you can choose your new best buddy by following the steps above.

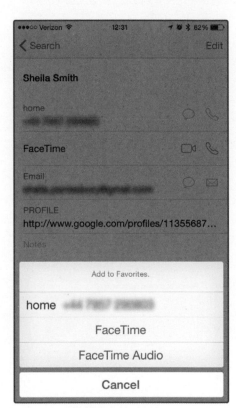

Above: It's easy to add a contact to your Favorites.

Adding More Than One Favorite for a Single Contact

You're clearly going to end up with three different numbers for many people and the good news is that you can also add multiple Favorites for a single contact. To create different Favorites for your partner's office landline, work mobile and personal phone, just repeat the steps above.

Calling a Favorite

It couldn't be simpler to phone one of your chosen people: just select the Phone app icon and then select Favorites from the bottom-left corner of the screen. Pick the person you want to call, tap their name and you're dialling.

Editing Favorites

Managing your existing Favorites is simple. In order to access the full list, simply tap on Contacts from the Home screen and then touch the Favorites button which appears along the bottom of the screen. From there, you will be able to carry out the following actions:

- **Delete a Favorite:** Press the red circle icon and then tap the Delete button that appears next to your soon-to-be-former Favorite. This won't delete them from your Contacts – only from the Favorites.

- **Reorder your Favorites list:** Just press and hold the icon with the three horizontal lines that appears next to the contact's name. While still holding, drag and drop it into the new position; press Done when you're finished tweaking the list.

Accessing Recent Contacts

iOS 8 builds on the multitasking experience, giving you quick access to your most-used contacts. Double-tap the home button when the phone is unlocked to launch multitasking and you'll see Recents across the top. Tap one of the circles to see the contact options.

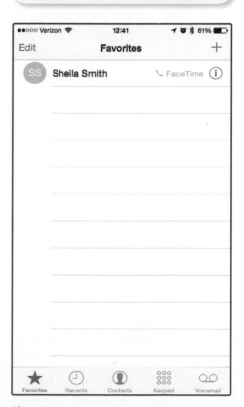

Hot Tip

Only want to receive calls from the special people on your Favorites list after 9pm or over the weekend? Select Favorites in the Do Not Disturb settings to filter out all other callers.

Above: Favored contacts appear as a list within the Phone app.

Above: To call a number if it's not stored in your Contacts, simply dial it by using the keypad, then press the green call button.

DIALLING

Time to make a call! Start by selecting the Phone icon on the Home screen and this will bring up the familiar number keypad, plus four other options along the bottom: Favorites, Recents, Contacts and Voicemail. You can then choose how you want to dial.

○ **Know the number?** Use the keypad to enter the digits, then press the green call button.

○ **Dialling a recently dialled number or missed call:** Tapping the Recents icon opens your call log, showing all the incoming and outgoing calls to and from your phone. You can filter these to show All, Missed or Completed calls. From here, you can touch the blue 'i' button to see more details of who called or tap the name to return the call.

○ **Dialling using Favorites:** Press the Favorites icon to call up all your personal VIPs and touch anywhere on their name to start dialling.

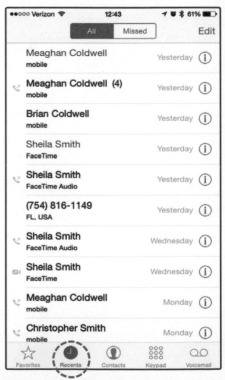

Above: Selecting the Recents icon on the Contacts screen displays all your incoming and outgoing calls.

- **Calling from Contacts**: Select Contacts from the bottom of the screen. Scan your address book by scrolling, searching or using the A–Z strip and then tap on the contact you wish to call to bring up their Contact card. From here, you can choose which number to dial if they have multiple entries (e.g. work, home and mobile).

Voice Dialling

Controlling your devices using only your silky voice is an emerging trend. Until now, it's been fairly unreliable, but advances in voice recognition technology mean that smartphones and computers can now decipher us better than ever. Apple's take on voice control – the personal assistant Siri – is leading the way.

- **Voice Dialling using Siri**: If you have Siri activated (Go to Settings > General > Siri), just press and hold the Home button until Siri appears and then say 'Call Bob'. Siri will launch the Phone app and dial for you.

- **Standard Voice Dialling (all versions)**: If you haven't enabled Siri, press and hold the Home button until the Voice Control screen appears and you hear a beep. Say 'Call' or 'Dial' and then say the name or number you wish to call. Remember to speak clearly and naturally – no need to impersonate a robot or a Brit buying a coffee in Paris. Use full names and add 'at home', 'at work' or 'mobile' where necessary.

Right: It's easy to make calls with Siri without searching through the iPhone to find the contact.

Hot Tip

Prevent voice dialling when the iPhone is locked. Go to Settings > Touch ID and Passcode and then turn off Voice Dial. After this, you must unlock the iPhone to use voice dialling.

HANDS-FREE

In the previous section, we showed you how to use voice dialling to make a call. If you want to make the entire conversation a hands-free affair so you can apply your opposable thumbs to more important things, such as holding the steering wheel or taking dinner out of the oven before it burns, here's how you can do that with your iPhone.

- **Put your phone on speakerphone**: From the Call screen, you'll see a Speaker icon. Tap this at any time during the call and the audio will play back through the iPhone's built-in speaker. Tap the icon again to turn off speakerphone and return to your phone's normal speaker.

- **Use a wired headset**: You can use the Apple EarPods that come boxed with your phone or you can buy a pair from another manufacturer. There are hundreds to choose from, but make sure you get a pair with a built-in microphone and a center button you can press to answer calls.

- **Use a wireless headset**: You can skip the cables entirely and pair your phone with a wireless Bluetooth headset. After you've paired it once, any time you're in range of your iPhone (and your iPhone's Bluetooth is switched on), your headset will automatically connect, leaving you free to answer and make calls without ever touching your phone.

Right: Call screen with the speakerphone option selected.

○ **Bluetooth:** Most new cars, built in the last five years, come with a Bluetooth-enabled media system. The principle for connecting your iPhone to this is exactly the same as a Bluetooth headset. Make sure your iPhone Bluetooth is switched on and then follow the pairing instructions on your car media system. Once paired, many car systems offer enhanced controls such as phonebook syncing and calls controlled via buttons on the steering wheel.

How to Pair a Bluetooth Device with Your iPhone

1. Make the device you're connecting with your iPhone discoverable.

2. On your iPhone, go to Settings > Bluetooth and switch on Bluetooth.

3. The iPhone will scan for available devices with which to pair and you should see your device listed. The name displayed will depend on what the manufacturer allocated, but hopefully it should be obvious. Select your device and, if prompted, enter the pairing code allocated by the manufacturer (see the product manual).

Above: The Bluetooth settings screen can be used to pair other Bluetooth devices with your iPhone.

Hot Tip

If you're prompted for a code while attempting to pair Bluetooth devices, try entering '0000'. This is very often the default code used by device manufacturers. Specific codes are reserved for products where added security is required.

Hands-free Siri

In addition to making hands-free calls with the standard iPhone voice control, it's also possible to use Apple's new voice-controlled personal assistant Siri to start and end calls, without having to touch your iPhone. You can also write and send messages, schedule meetings, get directions, set reminders and search the web, simply by talking. Siri works with the headset that came with your iPhone or you can buy your own compatible wired or Bluetooth headset.

○ **To start talking to Siri using a headset:** Press and hold the centre button on your iPhone (or the call button on a Bluetooth headset). Siri will come to life and ask what you'd like to do. You can then fire off instructions, such as 'Call Dave'.

○ **To continue a conversation with Siri:** Once you've got Siri's attention, press and hold the button each time you want to talk. When using a headset, Siri will respond to you via your earphones.

○ **Sending hands-free messages:** You can dictate text messages and emails via your headset mic to Siri. She'll read back your beautiful prose before sending, in order to give you a chance to ensure it's all correct.

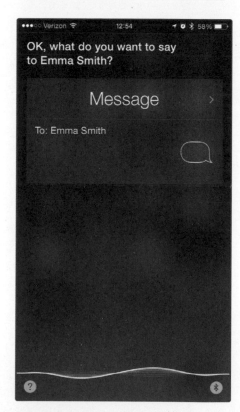

Hot Tip

The more Siri knows, the better. Create Contact cards for key family members such as Mum or Sister. Add nicknames, addresses and email addresses to help Siri respond better to your requests.

Above: You can dictate messages to Siri and send them without touching the phone.

CONFERENCE CALLS

A conference call allows groups of people to connect on a single phone call. They are mainly used for business meetings, but they also provide a great new way for families to catch up over long distances. Provided your mobile phone network allows it, you can create iPhone conference calls with up to five other people. Alternatively, for international calls, you can use services such as Skype, FaceTime or Google Hangouts over Wi-Fi. This not only saves money but also offers the added bonus of video calling.

Managing a Conference Call

Conference calls are often prearranged with a designated list of attendees and one person taking responsibility for 'chairing' the conference. However, the iPhone makes it very easy to bring people into existing calls, so you can also create a conference call at those unexpected moments when two family members call you at the same time. Whether you're the person inviting others on to the call or you want to connect people dialling in, here's how you turn a one-to-one call into a conference.

Above: Selecting 'Add Call' allows you to merge others into an existing call.

- **Make your first call:** For a prearranged conference call, you'll need to dial one of the people joining the call first in the usual way (see page 66 for help with dialling).

- **To add a second person:** While on your first call, tap Add Call and then make another call. Next, select Merge Calls. Repeat as necessary to add up to five people to the discussion.

- **To remove an attendee from the call:** People can obviously leave of their own free will, but should you need to eject someone, select the 'i' icon on the call screen and tap End next to the person's name.

Above: When you receive an incoming call, you have the option to Slide to answer or tap Message or Remind Me if you don't wish to answer the call.

○ **To chat privately with one person during the call:** To have a bit of secret sideline whispering with someone on the call, just tap 'i' and then press Private next to the person you want to speak to. Hit Merge Calls when you're ready to resume the conference.

○ **Adding an incoming caller:** If an incoming caller wishes to join the call, simply tap Hold Call + Answer, then tap Merge Calls and this person will be added to your conference call.

Hot Tip
Make friends with the mute button on your iPhone and use it when you're not speaking so you'll be able to cut out background noise. It also leaves you free to sneeze, cough or have a conversation in the real world without anyone knowing.

RECEIVING CALLS

Taking incoming calls on the iPhone can be as easy as a single tap, but with a little customization, you can tailor your phone to respond to calls in a way that suits you best, based on who's calling, where you are or what you're doing at the time.

ACCEPTING CALLS

Life is full of decisions, and each time your iPhone lights up, rings or buzzes (*see* page 46 to learn how to set your alerts) with an incoming call, you've been handed another one to make. Ultimately, what you do next rests entirely on whether you're in the mood for talking, you're too busy for chit-chat or you just want to be left alone. Whatever your state of mind, here are all the tools you need to deliver an appropriate response.

○ **Answering a call:** If your phone is already unlocked, just tap the green icon to answer. If the phone is locked, drag the slider to answer. You can also press the Home button to answer.

Rejecting Calls
We're here to help, not to judge, so whatever your reason is for rejecting a caller, here are the most straightforward ways to decline an inbound call:

Above: Tap Message if you don't want to answer the call, but would like to acknowledge the caller with a text.

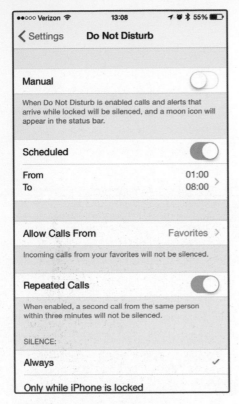

Above: The Do Not Disturb settings screen allows you to customize which calls you receive.

Hot Tip

The iPhone doesn't support call blocking. Silence persistent rogue callers by adding them as a contact, then download and assign them a silent ringtone. Next time they call, your display will light up, but that's all.

○ **Decline a call and send it to voicemail:** Tap Decline, press the Power button twice quickly, or press and hold the center button for a couple of seconds until you hear a double beep.

○ **Silence a call:** To ignore a call without rejecting it, press the Power button, flick the mute switch or press either volume button. You can still answer the call after silencing it, as long as you catch it before it goes to voicemail.

○ **Reply to an incoming call with a text message:** When the call comes in, tap the Message option (swipe up on the Phone icon, tap Reply with Message in earlier versions of iOS) and then choose a reply or tap Custom to send a carefully crafted brushoff of your own (to create your own default replies, go to Settings > Phone > Reply with Text and replace any of the default messages).

○ **Remind Me Later:** Remind Me Later is a handy feature on the iPhone that lets you reject a call but gives you a nudge in the ribs to call back when it's more convenient. When a call comes in, tap Remind to choose from 1 hour or When I leave. In earlier versions of iOS, swipe up on the Phone icon when the call comes in, tap Remind Me Later and choose when you want to be reminded.

Do Not Disturb Mode

Do Not Disturb was a new feature in iOS 6, designed to prevent unwanted interruptions. Of course, cutting yourself off from the world entirely would mean emergency calls or special loved ones wouldn't get through, but Apple has thought of that. Do Not Disturb can be customized to enable exceptions. Here's how to activate and fine-tune your built-in call buffer:

○ **To switch on Do Not Disturb:** Go to Settings > Do Not Disturb and flick the button next to either Manual or Scheduled. If Manual is switched on, it'll automatically silence the calls and alerts. Scheduled allows you to preset periods of time. Earlier versions of iOS just show the Scheduled option.

○ **To schedule Do Not Disturb:** Tap next to the From and To sections to assign times when you want Do Not Disturb to be switched on. For example, you may want to choose 'Quiet Hours' at night.

○ **To set exceptions:** Press the Allow Calls From button and choose from the following options: Favorites, Everyone, No One, All Contacts or a specific Group you've set up in your Contacts.

Hot Tip

Any Clock app alarms will still sound even when Do Not Disturb is enabled. In iOS 8, you can choose whether to always silence calls or only when the iPhone is locked

○ **Repeated calls:** If you feel like making an exception that allows persistent callers through, you can fire up the Repeated Calls option. If this is switched on, anyone who calls you twice within three minutes will be able to disturb your slumber/meeting/prayers.

Juggling Calls

The iPhone has various options that allow you to juggle multiple calls. Here they are:

○ **Put current call on hold:** Touch and hold the Mute button. Press it again to resume.

○ **Put current call on hold while answering a new incoming call:** Tap the Hold + Accept button that appears when the second call comes in.

○ **Ignore incoming call and send to voicemail:** Tap Decline.

○ **End the first call and answer the new one:** Press End + Accept.

○ **On a FaceTime video call:** You can either end the video call and answer the incoming call, or decline the incoming call.

○ **Switch between calls but keep both alive:** Tap Swap and the active call is put on hold.

If you're receiving a call from another iPhone user, you can tap FaceTime to switch to a FaceTime call.

Below: If you receive an incoming call while already on the phone, you will be presented with the below options.

RINGTONES

The iPhone comes with its own selection of chirpy ringtones, but the internet is full of thousands more and you can even make your own.

○ **Choosing a ringtone**: Go into Settings and choose Sounds > Ringtone. A scrollable list of available tones will appear. Tap any of the options for a preview; a tick will display next to the most recent tone you've listened to.

○ **Buying and downloading new ringtones**: From your Home screen, select iTunes > More > Tones; here, you can trawl tones by categories and popularity. To purchase, click the Buy button and the ringtone will appear in your available list.

○ **Setting tones for calls, texts, emails and updates**: To edit which sounds are used for incoming texts, emails and app updates, head into Settings > Notifications; here you'll see the options to change the settings for all of your apps, including Messages and Phone.

○ **Assigning ringtones to contacts**: Go into Contacts and select the person for whom you want to set a new ringtone. Hit Edit > Assign Ringtone and choose from the list.

Feel the Vibrations

You can also customize the vibrating alerts you feel when you get a phone call. Regardless of your tone, you can choose a different vibration at Settings > Sounds >

Below: The Ringtone setting screen allows you to preview and select which ringtone you would like. The selected tone will be highlighted with a tick next to it, as seen for 'Chimes', below.

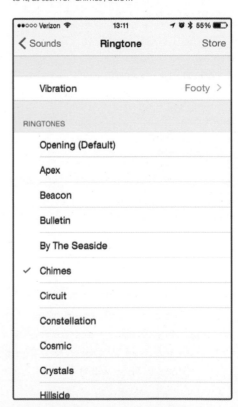

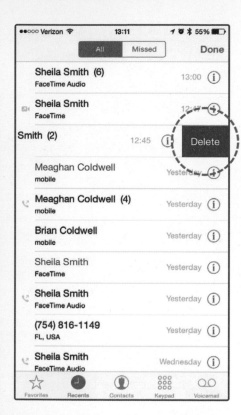

Above: Swiping an entry in the Recent Calls list will display the Delete option in red. This entry can then be removed from your calling history.

Ringtone > Vibration. You can select from the options, or select 'Create New Vibration', which allows you to tap on the screen and create your own pattern. For example, you could assign this custom vibration to a particular contact so you know who is calling even if the phone is on silent.

RECENT CALLS SCREEN

The Recent Calls feature on the iPhone lets you review calls you've made, received or missed and is accessed via the Recents icon at the bottom of your Home screen. This list of calls can be filtered to display All (every incoming and outgoing call, whether answered or not) or Missed (incoming calls you didn't answer). You can also access details such as when the call was made, how long it lasted and contact information for the person you called or who tried to call you.

○ **Call information:** Tap the small blue circle with the blue i icon to find out when a call was made, how long it lasted, when it started and finished, and any caller information stored in your Contacts.

○ **To return a missed call:** Simply tap the name of the caller and the phone will dial.

○ **To delete an entry from Recents:** Swipe any entry to the left and tap the red Delete button.

Hot Tip

If one of the calls listed is from someone who isn't in your phonebook, it's easy to add them. Just tap the blue i icon, followed by Create New Contact and fill out their details. They will then show up in your Contacts.

VOICEMAIL

Voicemail is an essential tool for collecting messages while you're otherwise engaged. Some excellent new features on the iPhone now make it even easier to set up and manage this tool.

SETTING UP VOICEMAIL

The first time you tap Voicemail on your new iPhone, you will be prompted to create a password and to record a custom voicemail greeting. Getting set up should only take five minutes; here's how to get your voicemail up and running.

Recording a Personalized Greeting

The iPhone comes with a prerecorded generic voicemail greeting (which will vary, depending on your carrier). However, we recommend creating your own personal message. Before you begin recording, make sure that you're in a quiet place and you've planned what you're going to say.

○ **To record your greeting:** Select Voicemail from the Phone app. If you have Visual Voicemail enabled (see overleaf), you'll see Greeting in the top left. Tap this and select Custom. You'll then be able to select Record.

Below: Greeting screen with the custom record a greeting option selected.

Above: You can select a password to protect your voicemail messages.

Hot Tip

Send an incoming call to voicemail by pressing the on/off button twice. If you're using the headset, you can also tap the microphone twice to send the caller directly to voicemail.

○ **To review your greeting**: You can review the greeting by pressing Play. If you're happy, tap Save or, if you want another go, follow the steps above again.

○ **Visual Voicemail**: If Visual Voicemail isn't available on your mobile carrier, selecting Voicemail from the Phone app will call your voicemail. Listen to the audio instructions in order to record and save your greeting.

Set an Alert Sound for New Voicemail

You can assign a specific ringtone to alert you to new voice messages. Go to Settings > Sounds and tap New Voicemail, but remember that if the phone is set to silent, it won't sound alerts.

Change Your Voicemail Password

Your Voicemail is password-protected in case you lose your phone or have it stolen. To set yours up, go to Settings > Phone > Change Voicemail Password. This is also the password you'll use should you wish to dial in and collect your voicemail from another phone.

New Voicemail?

Firstly, you should receive a notification that appears on your lock screen; secondly, there'll be a red badge on the Phone app, and thirdly, you'll see another red badge next to the Voicemail icon within the Phone app. Some carriers will also send you a text message when you receive a voicemail.

VISUAL VOICEMAIL

Forget wasting time listening to voicemails in the order they were left! Visual Voicemail now lets you see all the messages in your Voicemail inbox and select which you listen to first. No more wading through 10-minute monologues from family members when you really need that vital work update. This is not yet available on all carriers.

Visual Voicemail Explained

Below is a list of the main things you need to pay attention to while you're using Visual Voicemail.

- **Caller info**: In most cases, the caller's name and phone number will appear, but where no details are available, you'll see Unknown or Private Caller.

- **The blue dot**: This signifies voicemails you've not yet listened to. If it doesn't have a blue dot, that message has already been played back.

Above: The Visual Voicemail screen allows you to prioritize which messages you want to listen to or delete first.

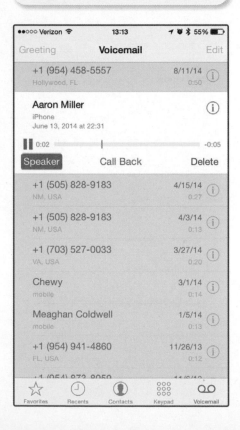

Hot Tip

The Phone app on the iPhone does not provide a way to save your voicemails in the long term, but you can download third-party apps like PhoneView on to your PC or Mac. These let you back up voice and text messages.

○ **Playing a voicemail**: Tap the name or number of the message you'd like to hear, followed by the Play/Pause button.

○ **Access contact info**: Tap the blue 'i' icon that appears next to the caller's name and number. From here, you can also add this person to your phonebook.

○ **Fast-forward and rewind messages**: Drag the progress bar to jump to interesting points within a message, just like you would with an online video. Something from the message you need to hear again and write down? Just toggle back.

○ **Returning a call**: Press Call Back.

○ **Deleting a message**: Press Delete. In some cases, it's possible to undelete a message if deleted by mistake, by scrolling to the end of the messages list and selecting Deleted Messages. Tap the message and press Undelete.

Retrieving Voicemail from Another Phone

If you don't have your phone with you, or the phone has run out of battery, you can still access your voicemails. Either dial your own phone number and follow the prompts (you'll need your voicemail password) or call your carrier's remote voicemail number. In both cases, you'll be back in a world where you have to listen to messages in sequence.

Left: Playing a message from the Visual Voicemail screen presents you with the options to Call Back or Delete.

FACETIME

FaceTime is a great way to bring people together over long distances, letting you see fellow callers while you chat in real-time, while Facetime Audio has also been added in more recent versions of iOS.

Below: While on a FaceTime call, most of the screen will show the video image of the other caller, although there will be a smaller image of yourself shown at the top of your screen.

SETTING UP A FACETIME CALL

There are a multitude of ways to set up a FaceTime video or audio call. You can use the dedicated FaceTime app, you can begin a FaceTime call from a Contact card or you can take an existing phone call and convert it to a FaceTime call.

1. Enter the FaceTime app and select Video or Audio from the top menu. You can enter a Name, Email or Phone Number in the search field to begin the call, you can tap a recent FaceTime call from the list below, or press the + icon to choose from your contacts. Remember the recipient must be on iOS or Mac to receive the call.

2. Head to a contact card (from any app; it could be Contacts, Phone, Messages or Email) and, if that person is available to FaceTime, a video camera and phone receiver icon will be visible next to the FaceTime menu. Tap one to begin the call.

3. Dial the person you want to FaceTime as if you were making a normal call (note: if you're FaceTiming someone on a Mac, iPad or iPod touch, you'll need to use the person's email address to initiate contact). Once the voice call is connected and you've decided to move to video, hit the FaceTime icon on the call screen. Once they've accepted, expect a short delay before their face appears on your display.

FaceTime Video calls

Once the FaceTime call is connected, in addition to the other person, you'll also see a smaller inset image of yourself on your phone screen. Three additional icons will also appear: Mute, End and Switch Cameras. The first two are self-explanatory; the latter lets you flick between the front and rear cameras – handy if you want to show someone something else in the room.

FaceTime Audio Calls

These are a relatively new addition to the iPhone scene and allow users to make audio-only calls via FaceTime, rather than video. This is great because it allows users to make voice-over-internet (VoIP) calls without charging it to your mobile bill. It's perfect for calling internationally over Wi-Fi and mobile data and it's great if you're in an area with a poor mobile signal but abundant Wi-Fi, as it ensures better, clearer call quality.

Blocking FaceTime Calls

You'll always get the option to decline a FaceTime call, but should you decide you never want to be contacted this way, you can disable it. Go into Settings, select Phone, look for the FaceTime section and ensure it is switched off. Once that's done, people calling you won't get the option of doing so via FaceTime (you can always turn this back on at a later date if you change your mind).

Hot Tip

For the last couple of years (iOS 6 and up), it has been possible to use FaceTime over your 3G/4G network, but make sure you check your data plan first or you could end up with a hefty bill.

Flicking Between FaceTime, Phone Calls and Apps

A big bonus of iPhone's multitasking skills is the ability to use apps while on a FaceTime or a regular phonecall. It's great if you need to check diary dates, grab information from email or find something on a map. To do this, tap the Home button while the FaceTime call is live and then navigate your phone as normal. When you decide to return to your FaceTime's mugshot, simply tap the green bar at the top of the screen.

MESSAGING

SMS (Short Messaging Service), or text messaging, has become one of the nation's most popular forms of communication, with an estimated 145 billion texts being sent in the UK in 2014. In this section we'll show you how to master the art of texting from your iPhone.

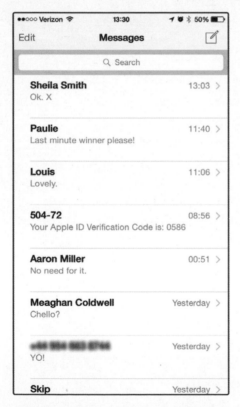

Above: The message screen allows you to send new messages, respond to messages and edit your message inbox.

SENDING AN SMS

Sending text messages on the iPhone is painfree but there are many different ways to achieve your desired effect:

○ **To send a new message:** Tap the Messages icon on your Home screen to jump into the Messages app. Here, you'll see a list of all your received messages and a pencil and paper icon in the top-right corner. Press that icon and type in a contact number, start typing a name or hit the blue + button to choose someone from your address book. Write your message in the field below and then hit Send.

○ **To respond to a message from an Alert Notification:** Press Reply to bring up the quick reply box (iOS 8 only; in older versions, you'll be transported to the conversation view), type your witty retort into the Text Message field and press Send.

○ **Banner notifications**: If you receive your text alerts as Banner notifications, you can also reply directly from those. When the message arrives, pull down on the little tab to reveal the reply field.

○ **Texting multiple people**: If you want to send an SMS to more than one person – let's say to share a change of location for dinner – all you have to do is tap a second time in the To field and select a second contact from your address book. Repeat this for everyone you wish to contact.

○ **To forward a text**: Hold down the bubbles containing the content you want to forward, select More from the pop-up and tap the Forward arrow, add a recipient and share away.

○ **Failed texts**: From time to time, you'll attempt to send text messages when there is no network coverage. You can still write these and tap Send; they will show up as unsent messages in the conversation view. To send them, you'll have to enter the conversation again when you regain network access: tap the red warning bubble and resend.

Above: You can reply to a message directly from Banner and Alert notifications. The screen here shows a banner.

Hot Tip

Want a speedier way to type texts? There are lots of apps, such as Swype, that replace the iPhone's keypad with smart input technology that can predict words as you swipe over letters rather than tapping each one.

RECEIVING SMS

Receiving and responding to incoming texts will be one of the activities you do most with your new iPhone. In this section, we'll show you how to spot incoming messages.

Alerts and Notifications

Your iPhone can let you know you've received an SMS by trumpeting out a sound, vibrating in your pocket, popping up with onscreen alerts, or all or none of the above. You'll soon find which works best for you.

Setting Up Your Alerts and Notifications

In order to manage your SMS alerts and notifications, go into Settings > Notifications > Messages; here, you'll see a number of editable options to customize your experience. You can also decide if alerts should be allowed to show up on the lock screen, or whether everyone who sends you a text should have the same rights as the special people in your Contacts.

Types of Alert

○ **Banners**: These appear briefly across the top of your screen and display the person who sent the message along with the first line of text from the SMS (this is optional). After a few seconds, onscreen Banners disappear automatically. You can tap the banners to interact with them, while pulling down on the tab will allow you to reply quickly (iOS 8 only).

Left: Text message notifications also feature on the lock screen.

Above: The Messages app icon displays the number of unread messages in your inbox in a red badge.

- **Alerts:** These appear in the middle of the screen. Again, they show who the message is from and an optional line of the message. However, you'll need to choose to either Close or Reply to these to make the Alert disappear. In iOS 8, hitting Reply will give you the option to reply to the message quickly without entering the messaging app.

- **Badge:** Just like Mail, Voicemail and Reminders, you can set your phone to display the number of unread messages over the Messages app icon.

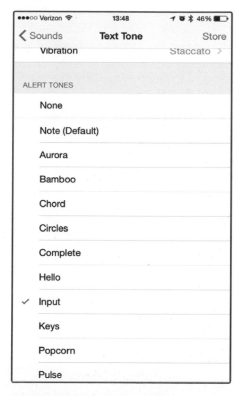

- **Tones:** You can assign one notification sound for all new text messages or choose a tone for a specific contact. If you want a general noise alert, go to Settings > Sounds > Text Tone and choose one of the listed alerts.

To Preview or Not to Preview?

You can choose whether you want the first line of a new text message to show up on your screen within Banners and Alerts. If you're worried about privacy, we suggest switching this off in the Notifications settings section.

Above: The Text Tone screen allows you to assign an alert tone to incoming text messages. You can also assign contact-specific tones. Selected tones are highlighted and ticked, as shown.

MMS

MMS (Multimedia Messaging Service) is the ability to send messages that contain photos or videos. Sending MMS messages is as straightforward as sending a text but it's worth noting that video and photo messages will sometimes cost more/use extra data, so it's worth checking your data plan before you start firing video clips across the globe.

SENDING AN MMS

Once you've mastered text messaging (see page 86), you are only a couple of steps away from being able to enhance your messages with photos and videos via MMS.

Sending Multimedia Messages

Follow the steps you would to send a normal text. To add a photo or video, press the small camera icon that appears in the bottom left-hand corner. You can then choose whether to add an existing video or picture from your gallery or to take a new one. Once you've made your selection, you can choose to write some text to accompany it; then tap Send.

Sending Photos and Video from Your Gallery

You can MMS photos and video while browsing through your gallery. When viewing an image,

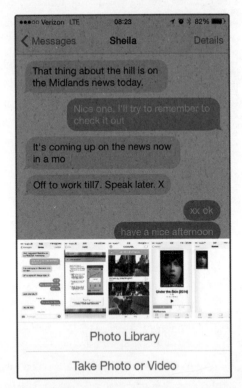

Above: Selecting the camera icon on the compose message screen presents you with different options.

tap on the Share icon in the bottom left (an arrow exiting a box) and this will bring up the options to share via your social networks, email and Messages. Just select Messages, choose a contact and tap Send.

AUDIO AND VIDEO MESSAGES

iOS 8 introduces a pair of wonderful tools for quickly recording and sending messages using the Messages app.

Audio Messages

The microphone next to the compose field can be used to quickly compose and send an audio message. Here's how:

1. Hold down the microphone and begin speaking. You'll see the audio meter running across the compose message field. When you have finished speaking, release the microphone button.

2. Preview the message by pressing the play button, delete it by pressing the cross or send it by tapping the Up arrow.

Listening to Audio Messages

Apple has added a neat trick with iOS 8 audio messages. When they have been received, users can simply lift the handset to their ears in order to listen.

Above: Hold down the microphone in the corner of the Messages app to begin recording a message. You can then send it.

Above: Just like a regular SMS message, you can view and interact with picture messages from an Alert notification. Tap Reply to type a quick response here.

Hot Tip

You can save images from the web and send them via MMS. Touch and hold an image, and you'll be given the option to save it to your Camera Roll or copy it to paste into an MMS or email.

Quick Video and Picture Messages

These messages are sent in a similar way to the audio messages explained above, only here, you hold down the camera button to enter the recording interface.

1. Select which camera (front or rear) by tapping the flip-camera icon in the top-right corner.

2. If you wish to record video, tap the red record button and tap it again when you've completed filming. As with audio, you can preview, delete or send the message quickly.

3. If you wish to send a quick picture, just tap the camera icon to send it immediately.

Receiving an MMS

Viewing MMS or picture messages is no different from reading an incoming text. The notifications and alerts follow the same principles and you'll see photos and videos you've been sent come up within the text conversation view. Small thumbnails appear in bubbles alongside normal SMS messages. A simple tap on the picture or video will blow them up to be viewable full-screen. If you like what you see, you'll also be able to download these photos and videos, by tapping the photo, pressing Share and selecting Save Image. This will save it in your Camera Roll.

iMESSAGES

Apple's Messages app offers special functionality for messages between iOS and Mac users. iMessages are sent using Wi-Fi and so they can be sent to any iOS user around the world without incurring charges.

SENDING AN iMESSAGE

You send an iMessage in the same way as you would a regular text. If you're sending a message to someone with an iPhone, their name will appear in blue in the To: field, and the message itself will show as a blue bubble when sent.

Receiving iMessages on Other Devices

Because iMessage is associated with your Apple ID, messages are received across all devices which are signed in to that account. If you have an iPad or a Mac, iMessages can also be sent/received on those devices, with conversations synced.

Sending Other Files

It's easy to share photos and videos through iMessage without risking racking up bills as with text messages. You can tap the camera icon to send an existing file.

From iMessage to FaceTime

The advantage of your iMessage contacts is they're also available to call freely via FaceTime. From an iMessage thread, tap Details and select the phone or video icons to make a FaceTime call.

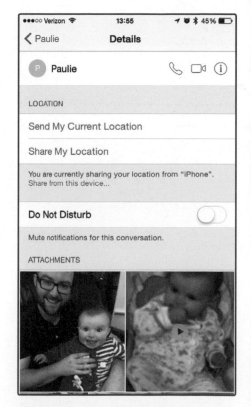

Above: It's easy to transition from an iMessage thread to a FaceTime video or Audio call.

GETTING CONNECTED

WAYS TO CONNECT

To access the internet, you'll need to be connected to either a Wi-Fi network or a mobile internet network. The iPhone can connect to both.

WI-FI

Wi-Fi is the wireless technology that allows you to connect to the web. The iPhone features the Wi-Fi technology similar to that on your computer or laptop, meaning you can easily access the web without physically plugging into the network:

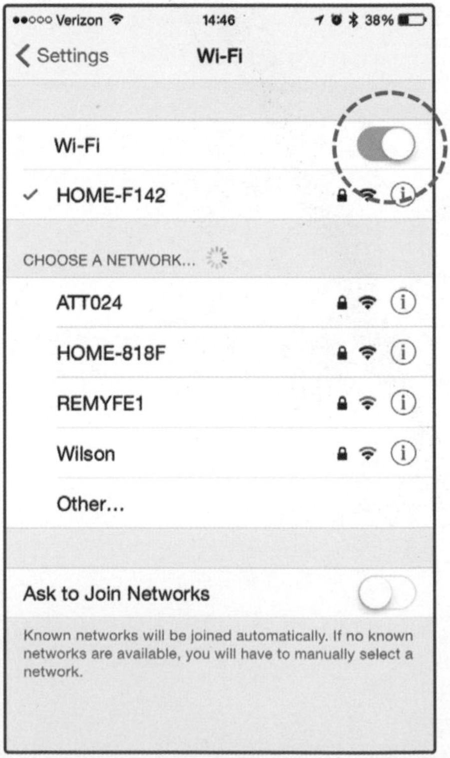

Connecting to a Wi-Fi Network

In the first chapter, we ran through connecting to a Wi-Fi network while setting up the phone (see page 26); however, here's how to connect to a new Wi-Fi hotspot.

1. Go to Settings and select Wi-Fi. If the Wi-Fi switch is set to off, toggle it on (you can turn it on/off in the Control Center).

2. The iPhone will scan your locale for available Wi-Fi networks. After a few seconds, you'll see available networks listed under the Choose a Network header.

Right: The Wi-Fi settings screen shows which Wi-Fi networks are available.

3. Select the network and, if it isn't password-protected, you'll be connected. A blue tick will appear next to the network and the Wi-Fi icon will show in the title bar.

4. If the network is password-protected, you'll be taken to an Enter Password screen. Type this on the keyboard. Once complete, press Join. You should now be able to access the internet. As a test, return to the Home screen, enter the Safari app and attempt to load a web page. If you're in a public hotspot, then further login information may be required.

Remembering Your Wi-Fi Places

Once you're connected to a network, your iPhone will remember you next time you're within range. So, if you connect to your home network, the iPhone will automatically pick up the signal and register your phone on the network when you get within range. The same applies at your local café or bar. In some places, you may be required to re-enter a password.

Ask to Join Networks

If you don't wish to log on automatically to a Wi-Fi network whenever you're within range, enter Settings > Wi-Fi and toggle the Ask To Join Networks switch to on. You'll then receive a notification informing you that a known network is available.

Above: Loading web pages in Safari displays them on your screen, allowing you to scroll to read text or view images.

Hot Tip

When you're in familiar places, make sure you're automatically connected to Wi-Fi so you can save on mobile data.

Above: Entering an incorrect password will prevent you from joining a Wi-Fi network.

Hot Tip

When deciding on which mobile data tariff to select, ask your network how much data you've used on average per month previously, but bear in mind that you'll probably be using more on the iPhone.

Wi-Fi Problems

Connecting to a new Wi-Fi network, especially if it's a public place, isn't always straightforward. Often, you'll see a notification claiming that you've entered an 'Incorrect password'. Before you give up all hope of connecting via Wi-Fi, check that you have entered the password correctly (are there lower or upper case letters that you have forgotten?) and ensure that the location you are at isn't experiencing internet problems.

MOBILE INTERNET

Although the world is rapidly moving in that direction, not everywhere you go will offer access to Wi-Fi. The iPhone offers advanced mobile data connectivity, which provides over-the-air access to the internet in the same way that you're able to make calls and receive texts.

Mobile Internet Allowances

When you sign up for a mobile contract, you'll be given a mobile data allowance by your network. Cheaper monthly tariffs will only offer around 250 MB to 500MB of data, which may be enough for light users. More expensive tariffs will offer 1 GB, 2 GB or even unlimited mobile data, which are more suited to heavy internet users.

Types of Mobile Internet

Depending on where you are, the speed of mobile internet varies a lot. In urban environments, you're likely to receive faster and more reliable internet connectivity than in rural areas. The current speed of your mobile internet will be reflected by the following letters and symbols:

- **4G LTE**: The most advanced mobile internet speeds are now available in most big towns and cities across the UK. To access these speeds, you may need to be on a special contract.

- **3G**: The most common third-generation internet speeds, suitable for browsing the web, using social networks, watching videos, and sending and receiving email.

- **E**: In some more remote locations, you may only have access to basic 2G speeds on the EDGE network.

- **Circle icon**: If you see a circle icon, you have no mobile data connectivity.

Connecting to Mobile Internet

Once the iPhone is activated, it will automatically connect to mobile data networks wherever they are available. You'll never need passwords to access these, as the data comes as part of your mobile contract.

Configuring Mobile Internet

While you will be connected automatically to the mobile internet, you can still turn it off or control which apps use mobile connectivity.

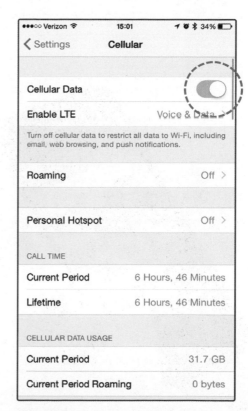

Above: Although automatically connected, you can choose to turn off the connection to your mobile internet data by toggling from On to Off in the Settings menu.

1. Enter Settings > General and then tap Mobile Data. Here, you can toggle the Mobile Internet switch to On or Off.

2. Turning off mobile data means that browsing the web, sending/receiving emails and downloading apps can only be achieved over Wi-Fi.

Mobile Data Exceptions

Within the Settings > iTunes & App Store, you can control whether downloads are made over mobile data or only when using Wi-Fi. This could be important if you have a limited data contract. You can toggle the on/off perhaps when you're looking to save data.

Preserving Your Mobile Data Allowance

As explained above, most mobile contracts now offer limited data allowances per month. Here are five ways to ensure you don't incur fees by going over your allowance:

○ **Use Wi-Fi**: Log on to Wi-Fi networks wherever possible and download large files while you're at home.

○ **Close apps**: Apps can use a lot of data by checking for updates when you're not using them (see page 164). Go to Settings > General > Background App Refresh to stop individual apps working in the background.

USING THE INTERNET

Now you're connected, via Wi-Fi or mobile data, you can start using your iPhone to access the internet through a web browser.

SAFARI

Safari is the web browser built in on the Apple iPhone. It is a mobile version of the desktop software that has traditionally been popular on Mac and PC computers. As it is one of the most used apps on the device, it sits neatly within the dock on the Home screen (*see* page 33). The icon is represented by a blue compass.

Loading a Web Page

To load a web page, tap the Safari icon on your Home screen. You should see a blank white page with a charcoal border at the top of the screen and another at the bottom. If you've used Safari before, the last website you visited will be displayed.

Below: Safari is the default web browser on the iPhone and sits in the dock.

Hot Tip

There is no need to type the www in the address bar; simply the name of the site and the suffix (e.g. .com, .co.uk) will take you to the page.

Hot Tip

There's a free, dedicated Google Search app, which offers a better, more comprehensive searching experience and access to the cool Google Now personalized information service.

Above: Typing a search term into the Safari search bar will bring up previous related searches.

1. Tap the address bar at the top-left corner of the screen, which reads 'Search or enter website name'. This will summon the keyboard. You'll also see a host of preloaded 'Favorites' like Wikipedia and YouTube. Tapping one of these will take you straight to that site.

2. Type in an internet address (e.g. bbc.co.uk, apple.com).

3. Press the blue Go button on the keyboard to load the web page.

Searching the Web

The address bar also allows you to search the internet. Start typing a search term (i.e. BBC Sport, Buy an iPhone) and press Search to load the Google Search results.

Finding Information Using Siri

Ask Siri a question and there's a good chance it'll find an answer from the internet (from companies like Wolfram Alpha and Yelp, to be precise) within seconds – and here's how:

1. Hold down the Home button for a second until the Siri microphone pops up.

2. Tell Siri your question, i.e. 'How tall is the world's tallest man?'

3. Siri will say 'I'm on it', 'Checking my sources' or 'Let me check'. If it can find an answer, it will load the information on a notepad, as seen in the screenshot to the right.

Searching the Internet Using Siri

If Siri cannot find an answer to your question, it will ask, 'Would you like me to search the web?' and you can tap the onscreen prompt or say, 'Yes'. This will load Bing search results for your query. Alternatively, you can just say, 'Search the web for...'. This command also works for Wikipedia.

NAVIGATING A WEB PAGE

Once you've loaded your chosen page, you can use the iPhone's responsive multi-touch screen to accomplish everything you could when using a keyboard and mouse on a PC or laptop – and a whole lot more.

Browsing a Web Page

If you're reading a news story on a web page, it's unlikely that all the text will fit on the iPhone's screen. You can browse a web page 'below the fold' by scrolling the page up, down, left or right with your finger.

Zooming into a Web Page

Unless the web page you're visiting has been optimized for

Above: Siri will respond to your question by rapidly searching the internet for relevant information and loading the answer on a notepad.

viewing on a mobile screen – as has been the case for many sites – it can be quite difficult to read text and get a close look at photos without squinting. Here's how to zoom in on specific areas of the page:

1. Pinpoint the area of the page you'd like to zoom in on and place two fingers on the screen. Push outwards with both fingers until you've zoomed sufficiently and then let go of the screen.

2. The second method is to double-tap a specific area of the display quickly, which will offer a precise zoom.

Hot Tip

To remove all the clutter from a web page (design, pictures, links) and make it easier to read the article, just click the Reader button in the address bar; only the text will remain.

Above: The SkyNews mobile website is specifically designed for mobile scrolling.

Clicking New Links

You can open an individual link on a web page by tapping a headline, category header or a picture. The new link will load in the current window, replacing the existing page.

Moving Back and Forth

To take a step back while browsing the internet, hit the Back arrow in the bottom-left corner of the screen. Likewise, you can use the adjacent Forward arrow to travel in the other direction.

Refreshing a Web Page

You can refresh the page to display the most up-to-date information by pressing the circular arrow in the address bar, thus reloading the current page.

Mobile-optimized Websites

If a site has been optimized for mobile devices, it will automatically redirect to the mobile site when you type in the address (for example, bbc.co.uk becomes bbc.co.uk/mobile). Also, such a site will not require any zooming and content will be neatly arranged horizontally for easy scrolling.

Opening a New Web Window

To open a new web page without leaving the one you're on, just press the two windows in the bottom-right corner of the Safari page. This will show the current open windows. You can flick between these or click the + icon to start a new page. This will launch a new blank page while preserving the first page; you can have multiple windows open at any one time.

Navigating Between Multiple Web Windows

In older versions of iOS, the icon in the bottom-right corner of the screen would feature a number, representing how many windows were open. This isn't present in iOS 8. In order to switch between web windows, tap the windows icon to show a vertical carousel of cards. Swipe between them and touch the thumbnail to select that page.

Opening a Private Web Window

If you are, for example, searching for engagement rings, you may not want that to appear in your search history and have the surprise ruined. To protect yourself, you can follow the instructions above, but select Private. No browsing history will be recorded.

Closing a Web Window

To close a web window, select the window icon in the bottom-right corner of Safari, then individually click the crosses in the top left of each window.

Hot Tip

When viewing multiple windows, turn the phone on its side to show thumbnails of the open windows. Tap a thumbnail to open a window.

Above: To close a web page, select the window icon in the right corner of Safari, then click on the individual crosses in the top left of each window.

Above: Clicking the Share icon enables you to bookmark favourite websites.

Adding and Accessing Bookmarks

Bookmarks allow you to store web pages for easier access in the future. It could be a favourite website or perhaps a link to a product on a shopping site like Amazon. This is what you need to do to save a page to your Safari bookmarks:

1. Tap the Share icon above the Home button and select the Bookmark icon from the popup Share screen. From here, you can add the page to a specific Bookmark folder.

2. Press Save to add the page to your bookmarks.

3. In order to access your Bookmarks, select the open book icon at the foot of the Safari window.

4. Tap an address to open that page in the existing window.

Sharing Web Pages

Easy sharing of web content is increasingly important to smartphone users, and Safari excels at this. You'll see the Share icon (the box with an arrow leaping from it) all over the place when using the iPhone and most of these tools are available within other apps, but here are the options when you select it within Safari:

- **Mail:** The mail icon will launch the Mail client with the web link copied into a new email.

- **Message:** Same as above, but in the Message client.

- **Twitter:** Share the link with your Twitter followers.

- **Facebook:** Post the link to your Facebook wall.

- **Add to Home Screen:** Adds an icon to the homepage for easy access in the future.

- **Print:** If your iPhone is configured with a wireless printer, you can print the contents of the web page.

- **Copy:** Copy the link to be shared elsewhere (into a document, a Skype conversation, alternative email app, etc.). In order to then paste the link, hold your finger down in a text box and select Paste.

- **Bookmark:** Saves the page to your Bookmarks.

- **Add to Reading List:** Safari offers a handy Reading List tool, which lives within the Bookmarks, allowing you to put together a list of pages you'd like to read at a later date. The Reading List screen is separated into two categories: All items and Unread items.

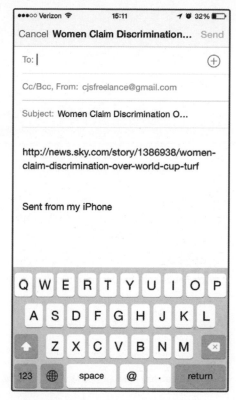

Above: By selecting the Mail icon from the Share screen, your Mail account will be launched with the web link copied into a new email.

Browsing History

Bookmarks and Reading List are just a couple of ways to access familiar pages. Tapping the Bookmarks icon will give you the chance to select a History Menu, which stores information about all of the pages you've visited in the past week.

Additionally, when you start typing a website into the address bar, Safari will begin to predict the page you wish to access, based on your previous activity (for example, if you start typing Goo..., then a list of activities related to Google may appear below). If you see your preferred site, simply select it from the list.

Other Web Browsers

Although Safari is the iPhone's default browser, there are other options available:

○ **Chrome**: You can download a free mobile version for the iPhone, which features a 'tabbed browsing' feature and enables voice search.

○ **Firefox**: The desktop browser made by Mozilla now has a free iPhone app available to download.

○ **Opera Mini**: Another browser, which is free to download and may be familiar to computer users; it promises faster loading times and mobile data saving.

Left: You can view or clear your past week's browsing history by selecting the Bookmarks icon and then History.

SOCIAL NETWORKING

The web continues to become more and more social. Services like Twitter and Facebook are among the most important ways of keeping in touch with friends and our favourite celebrities, and of keeping track of what's happening in the world.

FACEBOOK

Facebook now has over a billion users around the world and there are a number of ways to access the social network using your iPhone, so let's explore them.

Facebook: Built Into the iPhone

Facebook is built into the iOS experience, meaning that you can share web pages, photos and videos, and post status updates directly to Facebook from within various apps on your phone.

Setting up Facebook

To link your Facebook account to your iPhone and enable all the clever sharing functionality mentioned above, take the following steps:

1. Press the Settings icon, scroll down and select Facebook.

2. Enter your username and password into the fields provided, and then click Sign In.

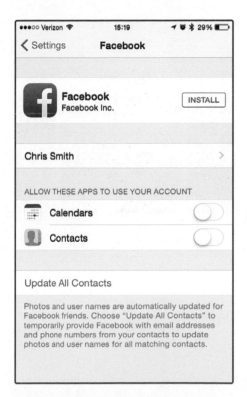

Above: The Facebook settings screen allows you to customize the way the app interacts with other iPhone apps, such as Calendar and Contacts.

Hot Tip

Don't have a Facebook account? Go to Settings > Facebook > Create New Account and follow the steps.

Below: Photos can easily be shared to Facebook by tapping the Share icon within the Photos app.

3. The next screen explains how Facebook will interact with your phone. Tap Sign In in the top right if you agree.

4. Once your username and password are accepted, Facebook will be synced with your iPhone.

5. Next, you'll get a notification asking you to 'install the free Facebook app'. You can do this now or later. Selecting Install will prompt a request for your Apple ID password.

Posting Status Updates

In previous versions of iOS, you could post directly to your Facebook wall from the Notification Center by dragging it down (see page 45) and selecting Tap to Post. This launched a unique Facebook dialogue box where you could type a status update and then select Post when you were done. As this option doesn't exist in iOS 7 and iOS 8, to post an update, you need to enter the Facebook app and select Post Update.

Sharing Photos and Videos

Once you've synced your Facebook account with the iPhone (see above), it's easy to post photos and videos to your Facebook wall.

1. Enter the Photos app and select Camera Roll. Scroll up or down to find the photo of your choice and click the Share icon.

2. Select Facebook to launch the picture or video within a Facebook dialogue box. If you wish, add a message to accompany the item and press 'Post'.

3. The photo or video will upload in front of your eyes and soon appear on your Facebook wall.

Sharing Web Links on Facebook

Safari makes it easy to share web pages through the Share icon at the bottom of the page. There's a dedicated Facebook button that enables you to quickly share interesting links with your friends.

Sharing to Facebook in Other Apps

As you download new apps (*see* page 159), you'll notice that a lot of them also incorporate the Share icon that allows you to share to Facebook. The YouTube app (*see* page 184) is a prime example. Other apps, such as Google Chrome, feature their own mechanisms for sharing, which also allow items to be posted to Facebook.

Share to Facebook (or Twitter) Using Siri

Rather than typing your Facebook message, you can have Siri do it for you:

1. Hold down the Home button to launch Siri and say, 'Post to Facebook.'

2. Siri will ask, 'What would you like to say?' and a blank Facebook post will load.

> **Hot Tip**
> In order to share a photo to Facebook instantly, take the photo, tap the thumbnail in the bottom-left corner to view it in the Camera Roll and repeat the steps above.

Below: You can use Siri to update your Facebook status.

3. Dictate your status update, e.g. 'I'm looking forward to the new Foo Fighters album'.

4. The text will appear on the screen and Siri will say 'I updated your Facebook status. Ready to post it?'

5. You can say Post or Cancel, or tap those commands on the screen.

Facebook Events in Your Calendar

We'll explain more about the Calendar app later in this chapter, but by syncing your iPhone with your Facebook account, event invites and friends' birthdays will be incorporated into your Calendar, which means they'll also appear in the Notification Center.

Facebook Contacts in Your Address Book

Integrating your Facebook account will automatically download your friends to your Contacts, along with any information they may

Above: If you have synced your Facebook account with your iPhone, your events will appear listed in your Calendar.

Hot Tip

Adding anything from 100 to 1,000 people on Facebook may make your Contacts a cluttered mess. In order to remove them, head to Settings > Facebook and toggle Contacts to off. The same applies if you don't want Facebook interfering with your Calendar.

have shared on Facebook (e.g. phone number, email address, birthday). In order to add your Facebook friends to your Contacts, go to Settings > Facebook, turn Contacts to on and then select Update All Contacts.

Installing the Facebook App

While you can access Facebook through the Safari browser, it's far more efficient to do so via the self-contained Facebook app. You may have installed this when syncing your phone with Facebook (see page 109). If so, a blue 'F' icon will appear on your Home screen. If you haven't installed it yet, access Settings > Facebook and tap Install at the top of the menu. You will be asked for your iTunes password; press OK and the app will install.

Using the Facebook App

The Facebook for iPhone app allows you to perform most of the tasks you're used to on the main site – here's a summary:

○ **Status/Photo**: Tapping these commands allows you to post a status update or a photo or video from your Camera Roll.

○ **Check In**: If you'd like to alert friends to your current location (e.g. home, a favourite restaurant, sporting event), tap Check In and select from the list of nearby places.

○ **News feed**: Launch the app and you'll see the News Feed with the latest posts from your friends. Tapping the posts will allow you to comment or 'Like', whereas tapping a name will take you directly to their page.

Above: The Facebook app can be used to update statuses, read the news feed, post photos and access notifications.

Hot Tip

If you have a notification that requires your attention, a number will appear next to the Facebook (or Twitter) icon on your Home screen.

Above: You can turn off and customize your Facebook alerts through the Notifications menu in Settings

○ **Requests:** This will display incoming friend requests from other Facebook users.

○ **Messages:** The Facebook app now requires you to install a separate app to use chat. Tap the Messenger tab to download Facebook Messenger via the App Store. You'll then be able to send instant messages to your friends.

○ **Notifications:** The alert bar at the foot of the screen will display incoming notifications from friends.

○ **More:** Here, you can tap your name to navigate to your own profile page, access settings and more.

Controlling Facebook Notifications

With likes, comments, photo tags and friend requests flooding into most of our Facebook accounts, you may not want those notifications to be delivered to your phone.

1. Select Settings > Notifications > Facebook to control whether alerts appear in your Notification Center, on the lock screen and determine the type of notification you'll receive (None, Alerts, Banners, etc.).

2. To receive some notifications and not others, you need to go into the Settings menu within the Facebook app and select Notifications > Mobile Push.

TWITTER

For those unacquainted with Twitter, it is a hugely successful and free-to-use social network that enables its near 300 million user base to post updates of 140 characters or fewer.

Twitter Integration with iPhone

Twitter has enjoyed system-wide deep integration with the iPhone for ages now (iOS 5 and up). It's easy to update your Twitter feed, to share photos, videos and web links, and also to receive notifications without even entering the Twitter app.

Setting Up Twitter

Setting up Twitter integration is a very similar process to enabling Facebook, which we explained on page 109. Head to Settings > Twitter, insert your username and password and press Sign In. As with Facebook, you'll be encouraged to install the free app, which can be done immediately or later. If you don't have an account, you can select 'Create New Account' and follow the onscreen steps.

Hot Tip

The Twitter app is continually evolving. To ensure you have the latest version, select App Store > Updates.

Above: The Twitter settings screen provides you with the option of downloading the free Twitter app.

Above: You can share photos via Twitter by selecting the Share icon in the Camera Roll. You can then add an accompanying tweet.

Sending a Tweet

Once you've entered your Twitter details or registered for an account through your iPhone, you can start sharing your 140-character pearls of wisdom with the world. In order to send a tweet, you should install the Twitter app. When you've opened the app, you can confirm your identity and your timeline will load. In the top-right corner, you'll see the paper and quill icon. Tap this to begin composing your tweet and press Tweet when you're done. Tap the photo icon if you want to add an image.

Mentioning Other Users in Tweets

To 'mention' a friend (or a user you follow) within your tweet, type the @ symbol on the keyboard and begin typing their username (e.g. @flametreetweet). As you type, the names of people you follow will appear to match your keystrokes. When other users are 'mentioned' in tweets, they will be notified.

Sharing Photos and Web Pages on Twitter

This is largely the same as the Facebook sharing explained on page 110.

Hot Tip

Adding a hashtag (e.g. #StarWarsVII) to your tweets will mean they will appear to all users around the world when they search for a particular topic. It's a great way to join the global conversation.

- **To tweet a photo:** Use the Share icon in the Photos app and select Twitter.

- **To tweet a web page:** Use the Share icon in Safari and select Twitter to load a new tweet, complete with a shortened version of the web link.

Above: The Twitter app displays your Twitter feed in an easily readable and scrollable format.

Both of these methods will summon a new tweet box, as mentioned above. As well as the embedded link, photo or video, you can add your own accompanying message, mention other users and add a geo-location.

The Twitter App

As well as sending out tweets, you need the free Twitter app for iPhone in order to read other people's posts, receive notifications, reply to tweets and direct messages, and control who you follow. If you haven't installed it yet, go to Settings > Twitter > Install.

Above: It is easy to add a new tweet using the Twitter app.

Using the Twitter App

As you can see from the screenshot, the Home section of the app is dominated by the feed of posts made by people you follow. They're usually a combination of friends, celebrities, companies or news organizations. Scroll up and down the screen to view more Tweets and tap one to interact with it. From here you can reply, 'retweet' (i.e. share the message with your followers) and add it to favourites.

Navigating the Twitter App

We've covered sending a tweet, attaching photos and mentioning other users, but there's plenty more you can do with the Twitter app. It has four sections listed in the navigation bar at the bottom of the screen, as described below.

- **Home/Timelines**: The main page, this displays your Twitter feed of posts from those you follow. Pressing Home again will take you to the top of your feed, and swiping to the left will give you a list of 'trending' (popular) discussion topics.

- **Notifications**: A list of replies and mentions of your username made by other users.

- **Messages**: Send and receive private direct messages.

- **Me**: Your profile page, complete with your own biography, tweets, profile pictures and the opportunity to alter settings and edit your profile.

Managing Twitter Notifications

Once you've installed the Twitter app, you'll receive notifications when another user replies to your tweets, retweets or favourites one of

Hot Tip

If you're adverse to the thousands of replies your celebrity status merits, you can turn everything off through Settings > Notifications > Twitter.

your postings, or sends you a direct message. These notifications can be configured and opened in the same way as Facebook notifications.

OTHER SOCIAL NETWORKS

The App Store offers dedicated portals to access some of the other more popular social networks (for a detailed guide to downloading apps, see the Apps chapter, page 152).

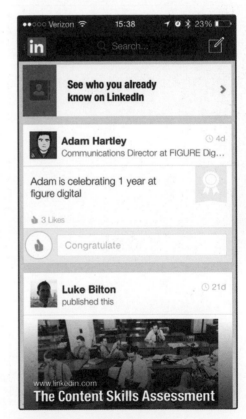

- **LinkedIn:** This professional social network allows you to showcase your CV and to connect with colleagues and potential employees.

- **Google+:** Google has launched a neat app for its fledgling Twitter/Facebook rival, but so far, users have been slow to engage.

- **Pinterest:** An alternative social network that simply allows users to 'pin' picture-based objects from around the web to their own 'boards'. It's great for creative types looking to collate ideas, shopaholics and lovers of funny cat pictures.

- **Snapchat:** A chatting and messaging app that allows users to send pictures, videos and messages to each other that disappear after a preset amount of time.

- **Tinder:** Looking for a date? Tinder is a social network for singles. Swipe right to like and swipe left to pass. If someone you've liked swipes right on you too, you'll be able to exchange messages.

Above: Use your LinkedIn app to connect and network with fellow professionals.

EMAIL

In this section, we'll talk you through the basics of setting up your various email accounts and the intricacies of sending and receiving emails using the iPhone's Mail app.

Above: Select your preferred email provider from the Mail app setup screen.

THE MAIL APP

Email is one of the iPhone's absolutely key pieces of functionality, and most users will use it several times a day. As such, Apple has taken the liberty of placing the Mail app in the dock on the Home screen, meaning it's always easily accessible. Select the app and let's get you set up.

SETTING UP YOUR EMAIL USING MAIL

Whether you're a Gmail, Hotmail, Yahoo Mail or Microsoft Exchange user, the Mail app has got you covered. When you first select Mail, it will ask you to set up an account and you'll see the screenshot left. Select the provider of your choice to move to the next step.

Configuring Microsoft Exchange

The iPhone is increasingly becoming the smartphone of choice for business users and, as such, it's easy to get your work email set up on the device.

1. Select Microsoft Exchange from 'Welcome to Mail'.

2. Enter your work email address and the password you use to access it. Fill in the description field ('Work' would make sense) and press Next.

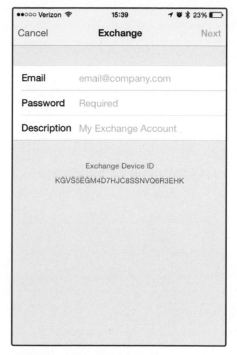

Above: Access work emails from your iPhone by setting up Exchange.

3. Once the iPhone has verified the login information, you'll need some information from your IT guys to complete the setup. Ask them for the Server information (e.g. server.company.com), your company's domain name and the username you use for the account. Once you've entered that information into the respective fields, press Next.

4. If you've done this correctly, you'll see ticks appear next to all of the fields.

5. The next screen features the opportunity to add information from your account to the Contacts and Calendars applications. There's more on this in the Calendars and Contacts sections (see pages 47 and 56).

6. Once you're happy with this, press Save.

7. Within seconds, you should see a batch of emails arrive in your inbox.

Configuring Gmail, Hotmail, Yahoo! and Others

If adding Microsoft Exchange email details seemed a little tricky and convoluted, don't worry, because setting up your personal webmail email is a doddle.

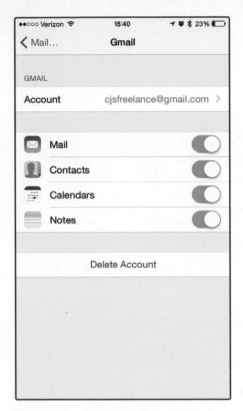

Above: Once you have configured your account to the Mail app, you can sync details such as contact lists.

1. Select your email provider from the list on the 'Welcome to Mail' screen.

2. If you've added a different account already, you'll need to select Settings > Mail, Contacts, Calendar > Add Account.

3. To configure the likes of Gmail, Yahoo!, Hotmail and others, add your name, email address, password and a description (optional), and press Next.

4. If you've entered the details correctly, ticks will appear next to all of the fields and the iPhone will progress to the final setup screen.

5. Once that's dealt with, press Save to start receiving emails. You'll also be asked whether you want to sync your contacts, calendar information and any reminders you've set using that service.

Syncing Email with Other Apps

Depending on which email provider you're using, you'll be able to pull in details to work with some of the other apps on the iPhone. For example, Yahoo! users can sync their Contacts and Calendars, as well as their Reminders and Notes (see chapter one, page 12).

Combined and Multiple Inboxes

Once you've added your accounts, you can access them through the Mailboxes screen within the Mail app (see screenshot right). Here, you'll see the option to select All Inboxes, which will show you all emails in the same inbox, regardless of which of your configured email addresses they were sent to. You can also select each inbox individually to see segregated Exchange, Gmail, Yahoo!, etc. accounts.

Email VIPs

The final option on the Mailboxes screen is to view emails from your VIPs (bosses, best friends, significant other, etc.). Select VIP from the Mailboxes and choose a specific contact from the Contacts app. These VIPs will have their own specific inbox, and you can easily configure special notification settings for their mails by using the VIP Alerts button.

DEALING WITH EMAIL

Sending and receiving emails using the Mail app is just as easy as text messaging.

Sending Email

Here's a quick step-by-step guide to firing off your first email:

1. Open the Mail app and select the New Message icon in the bottom-right corner.

2. Choose your recipient by typing the address into the 'To' field (known contacts will be suggested as you type); for example, joe.bloggs@email.com.

Above: The Mailboxes screen allows you to view your accounts individually or through a combined inbox.

Hot Tip

If you've received an email from someone to whom you'd like to give VIP status, click the name of the sender (highlighted in blue in the 'From' field) and select 'Add to VIP'.

Above: After choosing a recipient and subject, enter body text and select Send in the top right-hand corner to send a new email using the Mail app.

3. To select a recipient from your Contacts, press the + icon and select from the list.

4. Click Subject and type an email subject (e.g. Dinner?).

5. Tap the main body of the email, which says Sent from my iPhone, to begin typing.

6. Once you've finished typing, press Send in the top right corner. You'll hear a 'whoosh' sound once the email is sent.

Attaching Pictures or Video

Here is how to include a picture or video in your email:

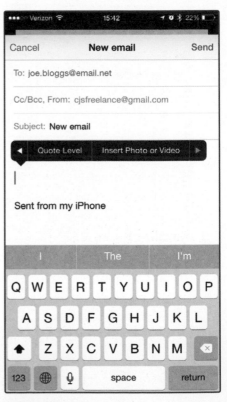

Above: Attach a photo to your email by holding your finger in the main section and selecting 'Insert Photo or Video'.

1. Hold your finger down anywhere within the body text field to summon a pop-up menu that says Select, Select all, Paste.

2. Press the arrow to the right of that menu and select Insert Photo or Video.

Hot Tip

In order to launch a new email with the photo already attached, select Photos > Camera Roll and choose the photo. Hit the Share icon and select Mail from the pop-up list.

Above: Siri can be used to send emails to people listed in your contacts.

3. Touch a photo from the Camera Roll to launch a preview and press Choose if you're happy. This will attach the photo to the email. Repeat these steps to add multiple photos.

4. Touch the screen to place the cursor above or below the photo to continue typing your email.

5. Alternatively, you can press the Share button within the Photos app and choose one or multiple photos (about five is the max) to load those photos pre attached to a new email.

Sending an Email Using Siri

As with Facebook, Twitter and Messages, you can dictate an email to Siri to save typing it.

1. Launch Siri and say 'Send an email to...', including your recipient's name. Siri will load an applicable person from your Contacts app. If you have many email addresses for the same name, it'll ask you to choose (i.e. Home, Work).

2. A cool postcard will launch, then you can dictate a subject and body copy and say, 'Send'.

3. Siri will attach a Mail stamp to the postcard and send the email. Simple.

Above: Swiping down an email message minimizes the window at the foot of the app.

Hot Tip

In iOS 8, you can swipe down to hide a compose-message window. This leaves it accessible at the foot of the screen and allows you to check other details before continuing.

Multitasking with Mail

As with all iPhone apps, you return to an app at the precise place where you left it. So, if you need to leave the Mail app while composing an email, you can safely browse to another app without losing your draft. When you return to the application, your half-composed email will still be waiting for you.

Saving Drafts

Alternatively, you can easily save draft emails until you return to them later. When composing an email, press Cancel in the top-left corner of the screen. From the pop-up menu, you can choose Delete Draft to discard, Save Draft to add it to the Drafts folder or Cancel to continue composing the email. Naturally, once the drafts are saved, they will live in the Drafts folder within your email account (see Mail Folders, drafts and Trash on page 130).

Receiving Push Email

The default setting for the Mail app is to bring in new emails as they arrive. This is called 'Push email' and it is designed so that it will continually go to ask the server if there are new emails, rather than the user having to refresh manually. When you receive a new email, you'll usually be notified by a sound (the 'ding' sound is the default) and a visual alert. A number next to the Mail icon on the Home screen will also show up new emails.

Hot Tip

If you find that having your work email and your personal email coming to the same app is a little too much to handle, why not download the dedicated Gmail, Yahoo! Mail and Hotmail apps from the App Store to help separate work and pleasure?

Fetch Email

While Push email arrives automatically, Fetch email instructs the Mail app to check for new arrivals at regular intervals. Select Settings > Mail > Contacts > Calendar > Fetch New Data. Turn Push off and select from the options under Fetch. You can choose every 15, 30 and 60 minutes or Manually (you'll only be notified of new emails when you open the app). Regardless of these settings, every time you open the Mail app, it will check for new emails.

Notify Me

iOS 8 has a Notify Me feature, which allows you to ensure you receive a notification on the lock screen if you're particularly keen to see a reply to that thread. When composing simply tap the bell within the subject line and select Notify Me. This helps to ensure you see the emails that really matter.

Scheduling Email Updates

Come 5 p.m. you may not want work emails but would still like to be notified of received personal emails. To that end, you can change the scheduling settings for each account. Here's what to do to schedule when the Mail app searches for new emails:

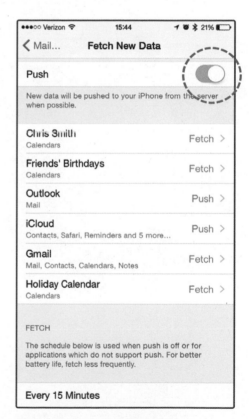

Above: You can choose whether you receive your emails by Push or Fetch. Choosing the Fetch option saves battery.

1. Select the Settings app and choose Mail, Contacts, Calendars.

2. Select Fetch New Data and then Advanced.

3. Choose the email account in question and select Manual. This will only bring in new email when you manually enter the Mail app.

4. When it's time to go to work, follow the steps above and change the schedule to Push.

Refreshing Email

You can manually load new emails at any time. From any of the menu pages (Accounts, Inbox, Sent, etc.), you can refresh by placing your finger on the screen and pulling down. At the foot of the page, you'll see a message telling you when the folder was last updated (e.g. Updated 13/12/14/ 12:35 PM).

Reading Emails

When you open the Mail app and select your Inbox, you'll see all emails listed with the sender, subject, first three lines of text and sent time. Any unread emails will be represented by a blue dot to the left of the message. Touching the preview will open the email. Touching the Inbox arrow in the top-left navigation bar will take you back there, whereas hitting the up or down arrows will take you to the previous/next email in the list.

Selecting Web Content from Email

Many emails will feature web links, perhaps from colleagues, friends or shopping sites, that require you to click to view more content. You can tap a hyperlinked picture or a line of text and the web page will instantly open within the Safari browser.

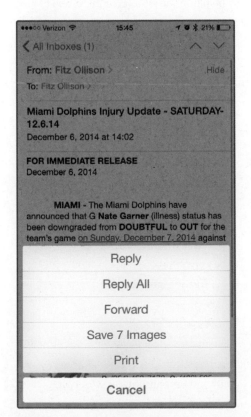

Replying to, Forwarding and Managing Emails

After reading an email, use the menu at the bottom of the screen to decide what to do next. The blue menu at the foot of the app gives you several options:

- **Flag**: Add a flag to the email to signal its importance or mark it as unread.

- **Folder**: Click this icon to move the email to a new folder (e.g. Receipts, Invoices, Favorites, Trash).

- **Bin/Archive**: Discard the email by removing it from your inbox and sending it to the Trash or your archives.

Left: After selecting the arrow icon from the bottom of an email, the reply screen will be displayed. You can then choose to Reply, Forward or Print. If there are images attached, you'll be able to save those too.

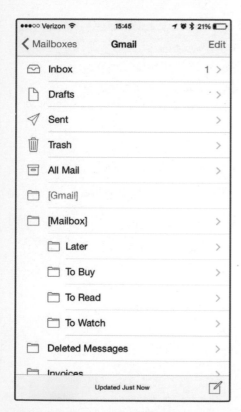

Above: The Folders screen allows you to organize and easily access different folders in your emails.

Hot Tip

In order to delete an unwanted email quickly, slide your finger across the preview to bring up a red Delete button.

○ **Reply:** The arrow allows you to Reply, Reply All, Forward it to a new contact or Print the email (if your iPhone is configured with a Wi-Fi printer).

○ **New Message:** From anywhere within the Mail app, you can hit the New Message icon to begin typing an email.

Deleting Emails

There are bound to be plenty of emails that you don't wish to read or store. Here's what you need to do to dispose of them:

1. Select Edit from within your inbox and an empty circle will appear next to all emails. Touching this circle will highlight it with a red tick.

2. Highlight all of the emails you'd like to delete.

3. Tap the blue 'Trash' button at the bottom right of the screen.

4. From here, you can also Move emails to new folders and Mark them for further attention.

Mail Folders, Drafts and Trash

Not all of your email activities take place within your main Inbox. There will be times when you'll want to access your Sent Mail, Draft emails and perhaps emails within your Trash that were deleted prematurely. From the Mailboxes page, select from the Accounts menu. This will take you to a list of folders where you can access Drafts, Sent Mail, Spam, Trash and more.

Conversation View

If you've received multiple emails from the same sender on the same subject (if you've replied and they've replied, and so on), you'll see a number in a square box to the right of the message preview. Selecting these emails will bring up a new page with previews of all of the emails associated with that conversation.

Mail Gestures

In iOS 7 and up, you can move emails to different folders and perform a number of other actions by swiping the message preview left or right.

○ **Short swipe from right to left**: This will present three options; Archive/Trash (depending on your email provider), Flag and More. More gives you a shortcut to Reply, Forward, Mark as Unread, Move to Junk, etc.

○ **Long swipe from right to left**: A pronounced swipe will send the email to the archive or delete it depending on which provider you're using.

○ **Swipe from left to right**: This will give you the option to mark the email as read.

○ **Customize**: You can customize these options in Settings > Mail, Contacts, Calendars. Scroll down to the Mail subhead and select Swipe Options.

Above: Swiping message previews left and right enables a number of options like Trash, Archive, Flag and More.

CALENDAR

Back in the first chapter, we introduced the iPhone's built-in Calendar app; however, in order to make the best use of it, it's better to have all of your email and social networking accounts set up, which we have done in the previous pages.

Above: The Calendar app will display today's date on the Home screen (here, it is second from the left, top row).

THE CALENDAR APP

This app sits on your Home screen. Touch it to see a monthly grid view, displaying the month, the year and an icon for every day in the month. Today's date will be highlighted in red. Tapping the date will show you a schedule for the day, including any birthdays synced from Facebook.

Navigating the Calendar App

Touching another date icon in the monthly view will take you directly to that day and show the appointments you have listed then. Touching an event will provide more details, such as the time, location, invitees and more. It is a little bit different in iOS 7 and 8 than in previous versions.

○ **Back arrow:** The arrow in the top-left corner allows you to move back to the month or year view.

○ **List view:** This option displays the month, and events for each day listed beneath.

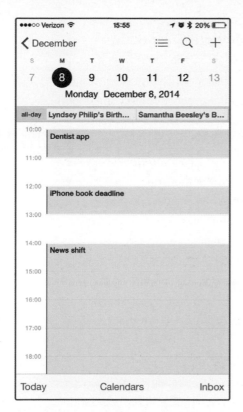

Above: Touching a date in the calendar app brings up details of appointments entered for that day.

○ **Search:** This lets you browse for calendar events.

○ **Add new event:** *See* page 136.

○ **Today:** Hitting this option in the bottom-left corner will always take you back to Today.

○ **Calendars:** Tap this to choose which of your Calendar accounts are displayed within the app (Gmail, iCloud, Friends' Birthdays, etc.)

○ **Inbox:** Here will sit any invitations you get to events, meetings or parties, etc. You can acknowledge them, accept or decline here.

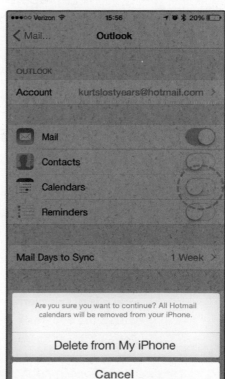

Above: If you turn off the Calendar for a particular account, it will be removed from your phone.

Hot Tip

When viewing the calendar in monthly view, days with events scheduled will have a black dot underneath the date.

Configuring Multiple Calendars

By default, the Calendar app features All Calendars. This means that it will feature events from all the accounts you've given the Calendar app permission to access. When setting up your email, you would have been asked whether you wanted it to sync with the Calendar app (see page 122). In order to select which accounts send events to the Calendar app, select Settings > Mail, Contacts, Calendar, then choose an account (e.g. iCloud, Gmail, Exchange) and switch the Calendar button to on or off.

Family Calendars

If you have enabled Family Sharing in iOS 8 (see page 191), you'll see a new Family Calendar created within the app. Tap Calendars and you'll see it right there. This links all members of the family. Users can also send Reminders to the whole family so they don't miss movie night!

Adding Facebook Events to the Calendar

Providing you've already added your Facebook account (see page 109), you can select Settings > Facebook and then allow the Calendar to use your account by toggling the switch to on.

Hot Tip

Enabling Facebook to access the Calendar app should set up a 'Friends' Birthdays' calendar within the app. You'll get a notification on the day and they'll also appear in the Notifications Center.

iCloud Calendars

One of the coolest and most useful iCloud features is the Calendar functionality, which syncs across multiple Apple devices. Therefore, if you make an entry on your iPhone, you'll see it on your Mac computer, iPad and even on the web-based iCloud.com page. To enable the iCloud Calendar, go to Settings > iCloud and turn Calendars on.

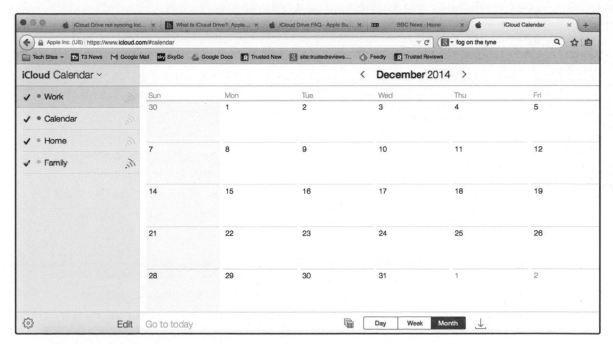

Above: Using the iCloud Calendar is a great way to view and manage your appointments on your Mac, and can be synced across devices.

Viewing Multiple Calendars

If you've configured multiple email accounts and allowed Facebook to push events to your iPhone, you can choose to view them all or just one at a time from the app's main screen just above the Home button. Pressing the various items in the list (e.g. iCloud Home) will add/remove a tick, making it visible/invisible in the All Calendars screen.

Searching Your Calendar

With all of these accounts pushing data to and from the iPhone app, it can be difficult to keep track. To search for details of a certain event, you can use the Search Calendars bar near the top of the app; tap and type to see events.

ADDING TO THE CALENDAR

The iPhone Calendar app will automatically sync with your various email and Facebook accounts (more on that later), but you can also add items manually – here's how:

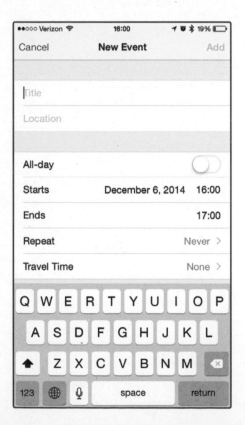

1. Open the Calendar app and hit the + button in the top-right corner.

2. From the new Add Event screen, enter the Name and Location of the event in the fields provided. By Location, you'll be asked to input an address or just use the Current location.

3. If this is an all-day event, toggle the switch to on. If not, select the Starts/Ends menu from the Add Event screen to add times by using the scroll wheel. You can also add a Time Zone, or choose to repeat the event. You can also build in necessary Travel Time.

4. Select Add to save the event within the app.

Left: Add an event to your Calendar by using the keyboard to enter the title, location and times. You can also choose to receive an alert.

5. Browse to the date of the event to see it residing within the Calendar.

6. Tap the event to see the Event Details.

Adding a Calendar Event Using Siri

Part of Siri's remit is to manage your Calendar, meaning that you can add appointments to your Calendar app and invite attendees in a couple of seconds. For example, you can launch Siri and say, 'Schedule meeting with Joe Bloggs at Starbucks at 5 p.m. on Friday.' If you confirm this meeting with Siri, it will be added to your Calendar app and an invitation will be sent to your recipient. You can also cancel appointments in the same way by saying, 'Cancel appointment with...'

Setting an Alert for a Calendar Event

Any Calendar app worth its salt will alert you when the event is approaching. When adding or editing (select the event and press Edit) an event, you can customize when you will receive an alert and select anything from None to two days before. You can also set a second alert closer to the time.

Above: You can schedule an event using Siri, who will add it to your Calendar.

Calendar Alerts in Notification Center

Calendar events are automatically configured to appear in your Notification Center, which can be accessed at any time by pulling it down from the top of the screen. This means that the events for that day will always appear as a constant reminder throughout the day. In iOS 8, they'll automatically appear in the Today section of Notifications.

Above: You can invite contacts to Calendar events by selecting Add Invitees and then typing email addresses or adding them from your contacts.

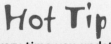

Hot Tip

Every time you update the event (time, date, notes), invitees will be notified by email.

Selecting Calendar Alert Styles

You can customize how you'll be alerted to all manner of Calendar events from within Settings > Notifications > Calendar. For example, select Incoming Events to choose the Alert Style (Banners or Alerts), choose whether it'll appear on the lock screen, whether it'll make a sound and show in the Notification Center.

Invite Contacts to Calendar Events

If you're planning a business meeting or a party, you can use the Calendar app to invite potential attendees.

1. From the Add/Edit Event screen, select Invitees; this will then load the Add Invitees screen, the iPhone's keyboard and a To: field.

2. To add an invitee, you can start typing the email address in the To: field. Alternatively, press the + icon to load your contacts. Selecting a contact will add them to the list.

3. Select 'Done' to send out the invites.

4. In order to see who has accepted, rejected or is yet to reply to the invitation, tap the event to access the Event Details screen.

Scheduling a Regular Calendar Event

If you have to go to the same meeting every week, you can schedule a repeating Calendar event. From the

Add/Edit Event screen, select the Repeat option. The default setting is Never, but you can choose Every Day, Week, Two Weeks, Month and Year (great for remembering your grandmother's birthday!).

Adding Notes to Calendar Events

To add details about the event, tap the Notes field and then use the iPhone's keyboard to type details; press 'Done' when you've finished.

Deleting an Event

To delete an event from your own Calendar (and those who may have accepted invites), select the Edit button from the Event Details page, scroll down to the bottom of the screen and hit Delete Event.

Moving/Extending an Event

You can change the details of an event by using the Edit screen, but there's an easier way too. Select the Day view in your Calendar and place your finger on the event bubble. You'll then be able to drag the event to earlier or later in the day by moving it up or down. To switch days, drag it to the left or right. When you've settled on a place, let go of the bubble. You'll also notice markers at the top and bottom of the bubble; dragging these in or out will change the length of the appointment.

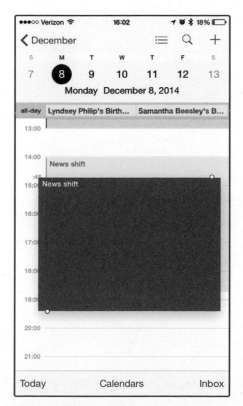

Hot Tip

In Day view, turn the iPhone on its side to view multiple days at a time.

Above: In Calendar Today view you move an event by dragging the event bubble up or down manually.

LOCATING YOURSELF

Whether you're searching for directions, finding a restaurant nearby or checking in at your favourite venue, you'll use the iPhone's mapping and location services more than you think. Over the next few pages, we'll explain how to get the best out of your new personal GPS device.

Above: You can switch on Location Services in your privacy settings.

LOCATION SERVICES

When you first set up your iPhone (*see* page 25), you will have been asked whether you wanted to enable Location Services and allow certain apps to access your geographical location. This isn't just handy for Maps but also for social networks, weather applications, shopping and ticketing apps, the camera, and Siri.

How Location Services Works

The iPhone can calculate your approximate location by using the GPS (satellite) signal, proximity to a mobile network tower and data from the Wi-Fi network you're logged on to. When Location Services is in operation, you'll see a compass arrow in the iPhone's title bar.

Enabling Location Services

If you switched on Location Services when setting up the phone, you're good to go; otherwise, it's easy to change. Head to Settings > Privacy and switch Location Services to On.

Enabling Location Services for Individual Apps

On the Settings > Privacy > Location Services screen, you'll also see a list of apps which are requesting access to your location. There are a few obvious ones, such as Maps, Compass and Weather, but also other less obvious ones, like Camera (in order to geo-tag your photos). Toggle the switches to On or Off for each app, depending on your preference.

APPLE MAPS APP

The built-in Maps app brings voice-controlled, turn-by-turn navigation to the iPhone, replacing the need for a dedicated sat nav.

Opening Maps

The first time you open Maps, a graphical map will load, with a blue dot surrounded by a circle, which represents your current location. If you're on the move, this blue dot moves with you.

Navigating Around Maps

You can move around the Maps app screen using a lot of the same gestures we've encountered in apps like Safari.

- **Scan:** Move around the map by placing your finger on the screen and moving it in any direction.

- **Zoom:** You can zoom in and out on any map by touching the screen with two fingers and moving them in or out. Double-tapping the screen with one finger will also zoom.

Above: The Location Services menu allows you to view and edit which apps are utilizing this service.

Hot Tip

To pinpoint your current location at any time, press the compass arrow in the bottom-left corner.

○ **Accelerometer:**
Turn your phone
on its side to see
the map in
landscape view.

Below: You can
view your location
and directions in
Satellite view.

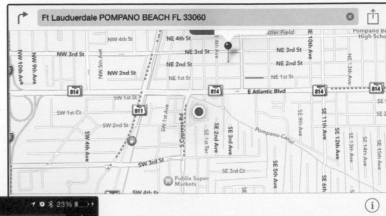

Above: You can choose to view your map in landscape by turning your phone on its side.

Changing the Map

As well as the standard graphical view, you can also access satellite imagery. At the bottom-right corner of every map is an icon (in earlier versions, it's a page corner); tapping it gives the opportunity to switch the view to Hybrid (as seen in the screenshot left) or Satellite, show traffic information, show the 3D map, drop a pin and even print the map.

SEARCHING FOR A LOCATION

There are a number of ways to search for a particular place (e.g. a restaurant, office, friend's house) if you're using the Maps app.

You'll find each of them in a tab above your map. In the next few pages, we'll explain how to use the Directions, Search and Bookmarks options.

Get Directions from the Maps App

Selecting the Directions arrow from the main Maps screen will load a new screen, allowing you to navigate from a Start to an End point.

1. Select your mode of transport (tap the car or walking options at the top of the screen).

2. The Start field will display Current Location.

3. The End field is blank. Tap within this to type your location. If that location is familiar, it will appear in the recent locations below the fields. If it is an unfamiliar location, suggestions will appear as you type. Touch one to select. If the destination does not appear, continue typing until the field is complete and then press Route.

Above: Enter your destination and touch Route to display directions.

4. A new Map screen will load, featuring your start point (represented by a green pin), your destination (represented by a red pin) and the route you'll need to take (represented by a blue line).

5. You'll also see a number of potential routes (touch one on the map to change it), with each giving you an estimate of how long it takes.

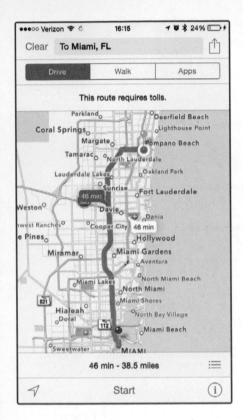

Above: The Maps screen will pinpoint your initial and final locations and display a route line between them.

6. You can use the blue dot to navigate your own way or press the blue Start button to launch voice-controlled, turn-by-turn navigation.

Finding a Place

Selecting the Search or Address bar within the main screen in the Maps app is probably the simplest way to find what you're looking for.

1. Tap the bar and begin typing your request. It can be an address or the name of a place, venue, restaurant, etc.

2. Familiar locations and suggestions based on what you've typed will appear below the

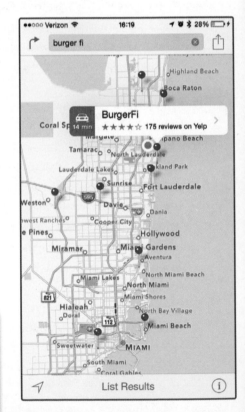

Above: You can search a location or venue using the Maps search bar. The results will show as pins on the map.

> ## Hot Tip
> Hit the flip-route button to the left of the Start/End fields to reverse your route – perfect if you're navigating the same route in reverse.

search bar. Tap a suggestion or continue typing and then press Search.

3. The nearest result (if you search for McDonald's, there may be loads!) will appear in the centre of the map, accompanied by a red pin and along with an interactive bar displaying the name of the place.

4. In order to convert the location into Directions starting at your Current Location, tap the blue car icon next to the name and then press Start to commence turn-by-turn navigation (see page 147).

Search Options

When you search for a location using Maps, you can tap the bar that appears next to the result (tapping the car will instantly load directions). This will display more details about the location, such as full address and phone number (if applicable), as well as the option to get directions to and from the location or add it to a contact.

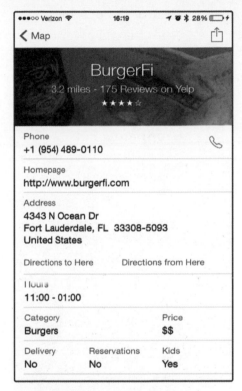

Above: Selecting the arrow seen in the screenshot left displays further information about the location, as seen here for the Burger-Fi Restaurant.

Directions to Favorites, Recent, Contacts

Tap the search bar to reveal a list of suggestions below. Here, you can select from Favorites (locations or contacts you've saved to a favorites list), Recents (recent places you've searched for) and Contacts (if they have a street address associated with them). Select any of these items to view them on the map and then press 'Start' to begin turn-by-turn navigation.

Adding a Favourite Location

In order to save a place to your Favorites list, select the Share icon in the top-right corner of the Maps screen. Select Add to Favorites in the bottom-left corner of the screen.

Sharing a Location

The Share location option sits on every Maps page. Tap it to see options like Message, Mail, Twitter and Facebook. If you've got AirDrop enabled, you can also quickly send it to other iOS and Mac users.

Dropping a Pin

If you're browsing around using the Maps app, it can often be easier to drop a pin on a location you intend to visit.

In order to drop a pin (purple in colour), hold your finger down on the area of the map; an address bar will pop up, enabling you to get directions.

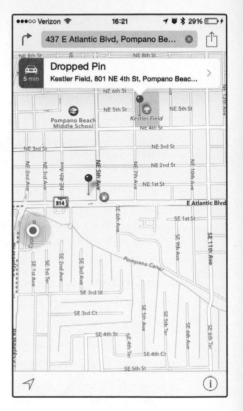

Above: When browsing using Maps you can drop a pin to view directions to a chosen location.

Get Directions Using Siri

Siri is neatly integrated with the Maps app to allow you to load directions within seconds. Launch Siri by holding down the Home button and request directions to a location; you can say, 'Directions home' or 'Take me to the nearest petrol station' and the Maps app will instantly load with turn-by-turn navigation. This will save you about a minute of typing.

Left: Use Siri to help you find your way; simply launch Siri and ask for directions to where you want to go.

MAPS' TURN-BY-TURN NAVIGATION

Just like an in-car sat nav unit (e.g. a TomTom or Garmin), the app will guide you from your current location to your destination with a series of detailed audio and visual instructions.

Using Turn-by-Turn Navigation

Press Start from any Directions page (*see* page 143) and follow these instructions:

1. Once you hit Start, the iPhone will issue its first voice command (e.g. 300 feet turn left on to Castle Street), while a visual road sign will display the same message.

2. Your position will be illustrated by a moving compass icon, which will move as you do. As you get close to your next turn, the command will be repeated.

Hot Tip

The iPhone's multitasking skills allow you to leave the app and still receive voice instructions. When you leave, the title bar will flash green with the message 'Touch to return to Navigation'.

Hot Tip

In order to navigate to your home address from wherever you are, tap the search bar and select Home from Current Location.

Above: Turn-by-Turn navigation is accompanied by voice instructions.

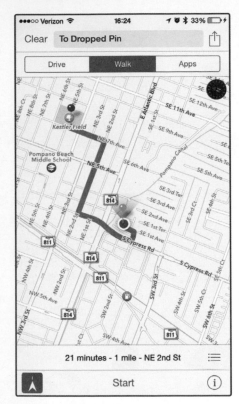

Above: The Compass feature is a useful way of getting your bearings.

3. When you're on the next street, you'll be told how long to continue for.

4. The next instruction will appear in visual form on the screen. Follow these instructions until you reach your destination. Once you're at your destination, press End.

Viewing Written Directions

To obtain a written summary of the directions, tap the List icon to show each step. If you're within the Turn-by-Turn interface, select List Steps to see a written overview of every turn you need to take.

Enabling the Compass

While hitting the Compass icon once in the bottom-left corner will take you directly to your Current Location, hitting it twice in quick succession will load the fully functioning compass. As you turn, the map will turn with you with the direction you're going in pointing to the top of the screen, making it easy to tell whether you're moving in the right direction.

Hot Tip

When searching for directions, you'll see Apps next to driving or walking options. This offers potentially helpful App Store listings that could help with public transport schedules.

Above: The 3D Map view allows you to get greater perspective. Especially of landmarks like Big Ben.

3D Maps and Flyovers

Tap the 'i' button on any map interface and where available, you'll have the option to view the map in 3D. This will display a slanted view of the map, which can help sometimes to offer a greater perspective.

In some major cities, Apple has launched a Flyover feature, allowing you to zoom around the cityscape. Where it is available, you will see '3D Flyover Tour of San Francisco' (for example) appear in the map, with an option to Start.

Other Maps Options

The launch of Apple Maps within iOS 6 caused quite a stir. Quite frankly, upon launch, it was a bit hit and miss, but it is getting better. Because of this, iPhone 5 users and those with older models who upgraded to iOS 6 have been turning to other options.

Google Maps

Google Maps had been the default Maps app on every iPhone until the iPhone 5, when Apple launched its own version to replace it. Those with newer phones can

Golden Gate Bridge

Above: Apple's flyover feature allows you to browse the cityscapes of several major cities.

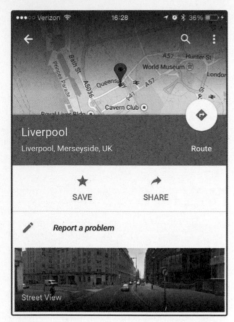

Above: Apple Maps is the default app on iOS 6, but you can download a free Google Maps app from the App Store.

download Google Maps from the App Store free of charge. The app offers fantastic voice search, turn-by-turn directions and the impressive Street View tech.

Traditional Sat Nav Providers

Afraid that smartphones were putting them out of business, the likes of TomTom and Garmin have launched iPhone apps with advanced features such as live traffic updates, regular map updates and advanced lane guidance. Search for Maps on the App Store to find these apps.

USES OF LOCATION IN OTHER APPS

As explained earlier in this section, the Locations Services is useful beyond map apps – here are some of our favourites.

Above: You can use iCloud.com to find your iPhone on a map.

○ **Find My iPhone**: This service enables you to use another device (an iPad, Mac computer or iCloud.com) to locate a missing or lost phone on a map, make it play a sound, remotely lock or erase it to protect your data. (*See* page 29, or go to Settings > Location Services > Find My iPhone).

- **Checking in:** Apps such as Facebook and Foursquare and a host of others (*see* page 118) encourage you to use Location Services to 'check in' at a location.

- **Exploring an area:** Many apps (Google+ Local, Yelp, Foursquare, etc.) use location data to let you know what's in your area, e.g. restaurants, hotels, attractions, petrol stations and cash machines.

- **Entertainment:** Apps such as Movies by Flixster and Ticketmaster use your location to bring you details of events nearby.

- **Geo-tagging:** The iPhone's Camera app (and third-party apps like Instagram) add a geographical location to your snaps. The location data will be identified in the Moments section of the Photos app. Tap the place name to load the location on a map.

Above: Check in on the Facebook app to interact with others and keep friends updated on your whereabouts.

Hot Tip

If you've enabled Family Sharing through iCloud (*see* page 191), you'll be able to track the location of your family members' linked devices. You can also start sharing locations, so it's easier to keep tabs on everyone.

APPS

BUILT-IN APPS

The iPhone comes with a host of built-in, or 'native', apps. From Maps and Siri to Mail and FaceTime video calling, there are plenty of tools to make life easier. However, the real joy starts when you add your own from the App Store. This section shows you how to enhance your iPhone experience.

COMES WITH...

The iPhone 'native' apps provide the basic functions for the handset. These tools are the backbone of your iPhone user experience and you'll get to know them well as you become familiar with your device. Here's a brief description of the main ones:

◯ **Calendar, Voice Memos, Clock, Notes and Reminders:** Great organizational apps we've covered throughout this book.

◯ **Camera:** The basic Camera app works with the iPhone's built-in cameras to shoot stills and record HD video. A new panoramic mode has been added with iOS 6 and there are additional editing tools now included.

Left: iOS 8 enables you to record video and audio messages directly from the Messages app.

○ **Contacts:** This app is your address book. It's a store for the phone numbers, addresses and contact information of all your friends, family and colleagues.

○ **FaceTime:** Apple's built-in video calling app that lets you chat face-to-face with other iOS and Mac users.

○ **Health:** Bundled into the iOS 8 models, this app gives you an easy-to-read dashboard of your health and fitness data. If you have an iPhone 5S/6/6 Plus, it'll also track your steps (see pages 157–58 for more information).

○ **iMovie and Garage Band:** Mobile versions of the great creative tools. These will allow you to piece together video clips or produce music on your iPhone.

○ **iTunes, iBooks, Newsstand and App Store:** Keep your handset fresh with new content via these store portals.

○ **Mail/Messages:** Essential communications tools for staying in touch with friends, family and colleagues.

○ **Maps:** Get yourself from A to B, whether driving or on foot, with Apple Maps.

○ **Music, Video and Photos apps:** These apps let you manage your multimedia content.

○ **Passbook:** Designed to help manage boarding passes, coupons, tickets, gift cards and passes by keeping them all stored in a scannable digital format in the app.

Above: Apple's Passbook app allows you to keep all of your storecards from places like Starbucks and even tickets from Ticketmaster.

○ **Pages**, **Keynote**, **Numbers**: Apple's own versions of Microsoft Word, PowerPoint and Excel are now built into the iPhone with iOS 8.

○ **Safari**: This is the iPhone's standard web browser. If you're an iPhone 5 user, this is optimized for the new 4-inch retina display. You can also auto-sync bookmarks and favourites across iOS devices.

○ **Siri**: Apple's voice assistant. This app lets you issue instructions and tackle tasks using voice commands.

○ **Weather**: Get hourly, daily and weekly forecasts for multiple locations.

Right: The built-in Weather app offers hourly and weekly forecasts.

HEALTH APP

Apple wants you to use your iPhone to be healthier, and with the new Health app that comes with iOS 8, you can be. Here's how it can help you to get in shape.

WHAT IS IT?

The Health app in iOS 8 is still in its infancy, but it is hoped that one day, it'll provide a comprehensive picture of your health and even provide information that can help your doctor. There are so many potential uses here, but we'll focus on a couple of the basic ones.

Dashboard

When you first open the Health app, you'll see the Dashboard displaying a number of graphs for things like steps, walking and running distance, and flights of steps climbed. As the iPhone's motion sensors can log this data it will automatically tally in graphs. You can choose the day, week, month or year view. Others can also be added in the Health Data tab.

Health Data

This tab is a little overwhelming just because of the sheer number of options. Many won't be relevant, but the idea is that Health speaks to other iPhone apps and accessories that gather metrics like blood pressure, calorific intake, sleep data and heart rate.

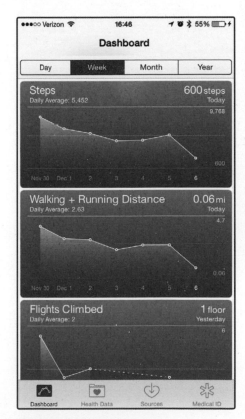

Above: The Health app tracks your steps, distance, flights of stairs climbed and much more.

Sources

This is where those additional apps and connected gadgets come in. Apps that have requested permission to update the Health app will appear in the Sources tab. Allowing permission will allow the data collected by those apps, for example, your sleep patterns, to show data within the Health app. For example, if you have a Jawbone UP fitness tracker, you can download the UP app, go to that app's settings and then enable access to Health. All of that data will then be fed into the Health app too

Above: The Medical ID you create in the Health app can be accessed when the phone is locked, via the emergency call screen.

Medical ID

One portion of the Health app could even save your life. If you open the app, you'll see a tab that says Medical ID. Here, you can add your vital information like your medical conditions, allergies, medication, blood type, organ donor status, emergency contact and more. If you add a Medical ID, you can also ensure it appears in the Emergency dial section of the phone so it can be accessed with the phone locked.

Apps that Work with Health

App developers are updating their apps all the time to incorporate Health. These include:

- **UP:** The maker of the popular Jawbone UP wristbands, which integrate steps, distance, sleep data and more.

- **MyFitnessPal:** Sends diet, exercise and weight data to Health.

- **Motion 24/7 Sleeptracker:** Monitors your sleep quality, snoring and heart rate and syncs it back to Health.

GET APPS

Although the iPhone has some excellent apps as standard, you'll definitely want to add your own. Before your start the voyage of app discovery, it's worth thinking about how you want to use your phone, how much space you have and how much you want to spend.

Below: The App Store is where you'll find thousands of brilliant and varied apps.

Apple ID

The App Store is another place where your Apple ID comes in handy. It allows you to download and purchase new content, while the password will also protect you from unauthorized downloads. We set up the Apple ID when setting up the phone, so your account should be ready to go when it comes to downloading apps.

Find Apps

Just like restaurants, bars or cafés, finding great new apps can be a real buzz. The main way to find out what's new and popular is by opening the App Store on your phone. Alternatively, just search the web or turn to page 250 for our guide to the Top 100 apps first.

APP STORE

You can buy and download apps on the move, from anywhere in the world, but before you can use the App Store on your iPhone, it must be connected to the internet.

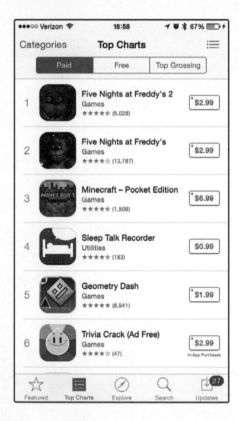

Above: The charts are a good place to start if you're looking to get some of the most popular free and paid apps on your phone.

CHOOSE YOUR APPS

Once you are connected to the internet, here is what you should do to browse the App Store:

1. Select the App Store icon on your Home screen to launch the App Store.

2. You'll see five tabs along the bottom of the screen: Featured, Top Charts, Explore, Search and Updates. Each represents a different way to discover new content.

- **Featured**: Displays a mini version of the iTunes App Store with selected content.

- **Top Charts**: Links you through to the Top Free, Top Paid and Top Grossing charts, showing the most popular apps of the moment.

- **Explore**: Browse categories and subcategories (for example, Reference > Astronomy, in order to be taken to a host of applicable apps.

- **Search**: If you know the name of the app, you can type it into the search bar.

- **Updates**: Clicking this displays any available updates for apps you've already downloaded.

APP STORE PRODUCT PAGE

Once you've established the app you wish to download, you'll be taken to the product page. Here, you'll see price (if it's free you'll see Install or Get, if it's paid, you'll see the price, if you already own it you'll see Open or Update (if one is available)). There's also a star rating, which gives you an idea of how well it has been received by the community.

Below this information sit three tabs:

- **Details**: This offers some screenshots, a description of what's new in the latest update and some information on the size of the download, who makes it and which devices it supports.

- **Reviews**: Read reviews from fellow iPhone users and write one of your own.

- **Related**: A list of other apps from the same developer or with similar content.

Hot Tip

If the word 'Get' appears next to the listing, it means there are in-app purchases available within the app.

Above: The App Store product page offers all the information you need before downloading an app.

Hot Tip

If you have an iPhone 5S/6/6Plus, you'll be able to use Touch ID to authorize purchases in the App Store. Go to Settings > Touch ID and Passcode and toggle on Use Touch ID for iTunes & App Store.

DOWNLOADING AN APP

Once you're convinced you want to download the app, tap the buy/install/get button. You may be asked to input your Apple ID password, but once that's been accepted, the app will begin to download. You'll see a circle showing the progress of the download and an app icon will appear on your Home screen, which says 'Loading'. Once it is complete and installed, you'll be able open the app and use it like others on your phone.

ORGANIZE APPS

You can have multiple Home screens on your iPhone and, depending on your iPhone model, each screen can hold up to 24 apps or folders. You can organize these apps to ensure they're in the most convenient places to access.

Moving Apps

Press and hold any app icon until the apps begin to wiggle. You can now move any of them on the screen: just press an icon and drag it to a new location or into a folder. You can move it to another Home screen by dragging it to the far left or far right of the screen.

Create Folders

Creating folders is simple: press and hold any app on your Home screen until all the apps start to wiggle, then press and drag the app you wish to drop into a folder on top of

Left: Placing similar apps in folders saves space on your Home screen.

another app you also wish to have in that folder. Give the folder a name (Games, Productivity, Photography, etc.) and you're good to go. To remove an app from a folder, just repeat the process and drag it back out on to the Home screen or into another folder.

Multitasking: Switching Between Apps

Rather than returning to the Home screen, finding the app icon and opening it, it's easy to switch between apps by double-tapping the Home button, then move left or right to find the card for the app you wish to use.

Web Clips

In addition to stuffing your Home screens full of apps, you can also add shortcuts to your favourite websites so that there's no need to open Safari. In order to do this, just open the site in Safari and click the + button, followed by Add to Home Screen.

Web Apps

Unlike normal iPhone apps, which are pieces of software downloaded to your iPhone, web apps are essentially websites tailored specifically to work on the iPhone but still live out there on the internet. You need to be online, but they have the bonus of not taking up storage space.

Above: Double-tap the Home button to access the multitasking view and swipe a card upwards to close an app.

UPDATING APPS

App developers will issue updates of their apps in response to feedback they receive via iTunes or to release general improvements.

GET THE LATEST

If app updates are available, a badge will appear above the App Store icon on your Home screen as well as on the Updates icon in the App Store. This will let you know how many apps on your phone have new versions ready and waiting. Within Updates, an Update button will appear next to the app that needs refreshing. You can either press that or hit the Update All button to do them all at once.

Remove Apps

You can delete apps from your iPhone by holding down an icon until they begin to wiggle, then you can select the cross on the top left of the icon and you'll be asked to confirm you want to remove it from your phone. If it is

Left: All updates can be performed at the same time within the App Store.

a game you're deleting, you'll be asked whether you want to keep the scores associated with the app in Game Center.

Organizing Apps via iTunes

Everything related to apps you can also do on your computer with iTunes. Just connect your iPhone to the device (either through Wi-Fi or USB), open your iPhone from the menu and choose apps. Here, you'll be able to remove apps sitting on the device, install ones saved to iTunes, rearrange icons on the Home screen, create folders and more.

Share Apps

Sharing apps between your iOS devices will be taken care of automatically, provided you're syncing with iCloud. You can enable this in the iTunes preferences on your computer by heading to Store and selecting Automatic Downloads. This will ensure all devices using the Apple ID will automatically have that app installed.

Above: You can delete apps by pressing down a finger on the Home screen and tapping the relevant cross.

App Settings and Preferences

The apps that come with the iPhone and the ones you download from the App Store have settings and preferences that you can edit. Every app will have its own functions available for customization, and there are two ways to tweak them:

- **In Settings**: Go to Settings and scroll down the page until you see a list of apps. Not all apps will appear here, but those with settings to change will. Tap the app name to take a look at what can be customized.

- **In the app**: Look for the words Options or Settings, or alternatively, an icon that looks like a cog. Failing that, there may be settings hiding within a More menu.

MULTIMEDIA

CAMERA

Your iPhone is a pretty nifty compact camera too. After reading the next few pages, you'll be convinced that you can leave your clunky compact at home.

STILLS CAMERA

The stills camera was once considered the iPhone's weak spot, but Apple has worked hard and improved it significantly over the years so that now there are few better smartphone cameras than on the latest iPhones. It will allow you to take 8-megapixel pictures good enough to blow up and place on your mantelpiece with pride.

Taking Pictures
Once you have selected the Camera icon on the Home screen, you'll see the world in front of you on the iPhone's screen. This means that you're ready to start taking pictures, with one touch of the onscreen, in-app camera button. Simply touch it once to capture the image in a fraction of a second.

Taking Pictures With Volume Buttons
The iPhone has never had a physical camera button, but in newer models, you can use the volume keys as a shutter trigger, rather than the touch screen. It can make it much easier to hold the camera steady, rather than straining to reach the onscreen button, especially on the larger iPhone 6 and iPhone 6 Plus.

Left: You can access the Camera app from your lock screen by touching the Camera icon and swiping upwards.

Taking Photos Faster

Photographs capture a fleeting, never-to-be-repeated moment, but by the time you've woken up the screen, swiped to unlock and entered a pin code or Touch ID print – and *then* opened the Camera app – that moment may have passed. Apple realized this and created easy access to the Camera app from the lock screen. Swipe this icon up to open the Camera app directly from the lock screen so that you'll be able to take pictures within a couple of seconds rather than 30.

Focusing in on Your Subjects

When you open the iPhone Camera app, the sensor will seek to focus automatically on the item in the centre of the frame and to give you a nicely balanced photo. You'll see a flashing blue square as the focus adjusts. It's wise to give the camera a second or so to complete this task before taking the photo.

Above: You can tap anywhere on the screen to bring up a yellow outline and make that area the focus of your photo.

Changing the Focus

Beyond autofocus, you can also tap anywhere on the screen to choose the precise area of the frame on which the sensor will focus. This is called tap-to-focus. Tapping this will define a smaller focus area, which comes in handy if you'd prefer to concentrate on a specific item within the frame or even something in the background.

Changing the Exposure

In iOS 8, you'll see a little sun icon next to the focus square. Drag this up and down to adjust the scene lighting. This will allow you to brighten up shots taken in lower light, but beware altering the exposure too much, as it will affect the quality of the photo.

Above: The yellow box indicates face detection.

Hot Tip

Rather than maxing out the zoom and ending up with out-of-focus photos, it's better to be cautious with the zooming.

Face Detection

Naturally, you'll be taking pictures of friends and family (or yourself). When the iPhone spots faces in a picture, it will outline them with a yellow box, meaning that extra focus is being placed on them.

Getting Closer to Your Subjects

On most cameras, there are dedicated buttons for zooming in and out on subjects, but this isn't the case with the iPhone, where any zooming needs to be done onscreen. In the same way you'd zoom in and out on a web page, use your thumb and forefinger to pinch in and out. This will also bring up a scroll bar at the foot of the screen.

Using the Flash

The camera on newer iPhone models (the 4S and 5 in particular) is very effective in low-light conditions and will produce better pictures than you'd expect. However, there are times when using the flash is unavoidable. You'll see an icon in the top-left corner which says Auto, meaning that the iPhone will employ the flash at its discretion. You can tap this to override and turn the flash on or off.

Taking 'Selfies'

While the overriding purpose of the front-facing camera is for video chat (see page 83), it's also great for self-portraits and group shots when the photographer is also in the frame. Touch the flip-camera icon in the top-right corner of the screen and take a photo as normal. The front-facing camera is not as good as the one on the rear, but can still take decent snaps and removes the guesswork from self-portraits.

OTHER PHOTO OPTIONS

Apple has spent a lot of time improving the camera options on the iPhone, and there are now quite a few tricks at iPhone users' disposal. The various shooting options are displayed in a carousel beneath the frame. You can move between them by swiping left and right anywhere on the shooting screen. The default, of course, is photo.

Below: You can swipe over to the 'Square' shooting mode to frame your photo differently.

Above: The iPhone camera options allow you to choose between photo and video settings, add filters, view previous photos and more.

Square

The next available photo mode is Square (one option to the right). This changes the aspect ratio of the photo to, you guessed it, a square. This is handy if you intend to upload the photo to Instagram, which uses a Polaroid-style square framing.

Panoramas (Pano)

You can capture a sweeping landscape or a massive family photo with the Pano setting. This requires little more than a steady hand, and the process can take a few tries to perfect.

Step 2: Once you press the camera button, the first shot of the panorama appears in the indicator.

1. Swipe right within the camera interface to get to Pano. Hold the phone upright (panoramas will not work well if taken in landscape).

2. Position the phone at the left edge of where you'd like the panorama to begin and press the camera trigger button. The first shot in the sequence will appear in the indicator.

Step 4: The arrow and the yellow line indicate vertical movement, helping you to keep your panorama even.

3. As steadily as possible (use a tripod if you have one), pan the camera to the right, trying to keep the arrow in the centre of the spirit level-type indicator. The progress of the scene will be depicted within the indicator.

4. When you've completed the entire shot, hit Capture again. You can view the results by tapping the thumbnail in the bottom-left corner.

Hot Tip

It's also possible to take portrait earth-to-sky panoramas by turning the device on its side.

Above: Completed panoramas can offer a unique perspective of your surroundings.

High Dynamic Range

Switching on HDR can offer much better photos in some circumstances. In simple terms, it takes a photo at three exposure settings – Underexposed, Overexposed and Normal – and combines the best elements of all three. When using this mode, a copy of the original photo will also be saved. The HDR option sits at the top of the screen when in Photo and Square modes.

Photo Filters

The iPhone now offers a select number of live photo filters that allow you to change the appearance of your photo before you take it. Tapping the filters icon in the bottom-right corner of the screen shows a grid of thumbnails, each showing how your current scene will look with that filter applied.

Timer

The iPhone camera has a timer option at the top of the display. Tapping this will allow you to set a three- or 10-second interval before the photo is taken. Just enough time to get yourself into that group shot!

RECORDING VIDEO

Any smartphone worth its salt is now capable of recording high definition video All newer iPhones can record full HD video which matches what's on offer from some dedicated camcorders. The newest models feature great slow motion and time-lapse video modes too!

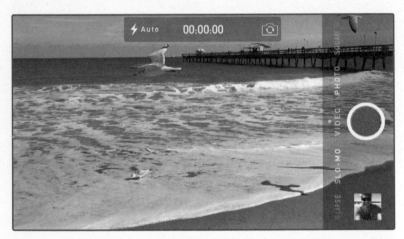

Above: The iPhone can shoot fantastic HD video.

Hot Tip

As with Photo mode, you can zoom in/out and set the focus and exposure. Video also boasts a facial recognition mode.

How to Record Video

There is no dedicated icon for the iPhone's video camera; instead, it's easily accessible from inside the Camera app. Swipe (one step right from Photo) and you'll switch to Video mode. A timer logs how long you've been recording.

Take Stills While Recording Video

Even if you're shooting video of a gleeful youngster blowing out his birthday candles, the iPhone's camera is capable of performing double duty by capturing still shots. After pressing the Record button, you'll see the stills camera icon pop up next to it. Touch this to save a still shot to your Camera Roll. Best of all, the shutter won't make its usual clicking sound and disturb your video.

Slow-motion Video

If you have an iPhone 5S, 6 or 6 Plus, you can shoot slow-motion video on your device. You can shoot at 120-frames per second, or if you have an iPhone 6/6 Plus, you can shoot at 240fps. For context, a normal-speed video is captured at 30fps. So, when recording at the higher frame rate, video is slowed down considerably. This looks great when capturing action videos.

Shooting in Slo-Mo mode

Swipe over to Slo-Mo and select your frame rate, then simply hit the Capture button and record as normal until you've captured your footage. Then select the thumbnail icon to play

it back. You can adjust the sliders to determine which elements of the clip appear in Slo-Mo.

Timelapse Mode

This is a new feature in iOS 8 and is available on the iPhone 5S/6/6 Plus models. When shooting in the Timelapse mode, the phone effectively takes a still photo at 'dynamically selected intervals', then

Above: Record timelapse videos to condense a few minutes of action into a few seconds of video. Great for sunsets!

stitches the results together in a video. The result enables you to see action captured over a number of minutes condensed into a few seconds. This works great for capturing a sunrise or sunset or perhaps a bike ride or car journey.

Lighting Your Video Subjects

You'll notice on the video capture screen that the flash options are still present. When shooting video, the flash turns into a light, which allows you to still shoot decent-quality video in the dark.

STORING AND VIEWING PHOTOS AND VIDEOS

Once you have taken lots of lovely photos and captured precious moments on video, you will want to show them to others, and make sure they are stored away safely in case something should happen to your iPhone.

CAMERA ROLL

After you've taken a photo or recorded a video, it'll leap into thumbnail icon in the bottom-left corner. This is your Camera Roll, where all of your recordings are automatically stored on your iPhone's internal memory. This is accessible in many different ways:

1. Press the thumbnail from within the photo capture screen to take you to the last shot. This is great if you're looking to share or edit a picture instantly. You can swipe left or right to move between shots.

2. Select the Photos app from the Home screen to access the Camera Roll (featuring thumbnails of all of your photos and videos sorted into Collections) and other albums you may have created (see opposite). Touch a thumbnail to begin interacting with it.

Left: The Collections section separates photos taken in different locations. Click on a thumbnail to edit or share.

Backing Up Photos

Your precious memories are safeguarded whenever you back up your iPhone: physically via iTunes or over the web via iCloud (*see* page 28 for iCloud backup instructions).

Storing Photos with iPhoto (Mac Users Only)

If you use an Apple Mac computer, you can easily import your iPhone photos and keep them on your computer hard drive. When you plug your iPhone in via the USB cable, iPhoto should load with the iPhone's photo library present. Press 'Import' to add them to your iPhoto library. Also, if you're an iCloud user, your iPhone photos should automatically land in iPhoto in monthly photo stream folders.

Creating Photo Albums on Your iPhone

After a while, your Camera Roll can become very cluttered; you can then create photo albums to group together certain events.

1. Select the Photos app, select Albums and hit the + button in the top-left corner.

2. Name the album and you'll be taken to the Camera Roll.

3. Tap the thumbnails to add blue ticks next to each photo and press Done when you have finished. A new album will appear in the Photos app.

4. In order to add more photos to the new album, enter the Camera Roll, tap Select, choose your photos, tap Add To and then pick an album from the list.

Step 3 (right): Select photos from your Camera Roll to add to an album.

Hot Tip

Rather than zooming in extremely close on a subject when taking the photo, keep the shot relatively wide and crop afterwards for the perfect proportions.

Above: Straighten out wonky photos.

EDITING PHOTOS

Taking photos and recording video on the iPhone is just the start. They can be fine-tuned using a number of apps and then easily shared with friends and, indeed, the world at large.

Editing Pictures Using the Photos App

The Photos app features a few built-in editing tools that allow you to fine-tune your photos before sharing or printing them. Select a picture from your Camera Roll or an album and select Edit in the top-right corner. The options that appear are the following:

- **Auto Enhance:** Tap the magic wand to magically adjust the colours and lighting in your photo. It doesn't always work, but in many cases, it's a quick fix.

- **Crop:** Cut out unwanted elements by dragging the Crop tool in and out. Here, you can also change the aspect radio, straighten the photo and rotate it in increments of 90 degrees.

- **Filter:** The live filters mentioned earlier can also be added after the fact. Add a filter to give the photo a different look and feel.

- **Colour and Lighting:** Select Light, Color or B&W to adjust the intensity of the effect by sliding left and right.

When you've completed the edits, press Done at the bottom or Cancel to return the photo to its original state.

More iPhone Editing Apps

The built-in photo-editing tools on the iPhone are very limited. However, there's a host of downloadable applications that offer much more flexibility when editing the look and feel of your photo before you share it. The likes of Camera+ and Photoshop Touch are great options to consider, while the photo-sharing network Instagram has a wealth of editing tools.

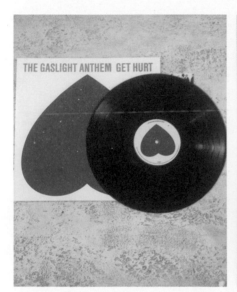

Above: Use the free Instagram app to take ordinary photos and give them a little extra flair through cropping and filters

SHARING PHOTOS

Throughout the second and third chapters, we've explained how to share photos through email, Messages, Facebook and Twitter, via the Share icon that appears whenever you're viewing a photo in the Photos app. There are a few more options, however, that we have yet to encounter when you press the Share icon.

○ **Use as Wallpaper:** Bored of the Apple default wallpapers? You can easily set images from your Camera Roll (favourite place, dog, family, etc.) as your background. Scale the photo to your preferences and select Wallpaper, Lock Screen – or both.

○ **Print:** If your iPhone is configured to work with a Wi-Fi printer, you can instantly print off a snap from your Photos app.

○ **Assign to Contact:** Got a photo you'd like to see every time you get a call or email from a contact? Select this option and match it up with a contact when the app pops up.

○ **Copy:** Tap this to paste the photo within another application, such as a third-party email app like Gmail that doesn't sit within the Share menu.

Above: The Photo sharing screen presents you with options such as setting an image as your wallpaper.

iCLOUD PHOTO LIBRARY

With iOS 8, Apple launched iCloud Photo Library. This is slightly different to Photo Stream. It allows you to automatically upload and store your entire library in iCloud and make it accessible on all of your iCloud-enabled devices. Enabling iCloud Photo Library (Settings > iCloud) will use your free 5 GB of storage. If you need more, you can purchase it from one of the monthly plans, which start at 79p a month for 20 GB.

MY PHOTO STREAM

Photo Stream is the part of iCloud that is responsible for syncing and backing up your photos. It is one of the very best reasons for enabling iCloud when you set up your device. If you enable Photo Stream (Settings > iCloud > My Photo Stream), every picture you take using your iPhone will be automatically uploaded to iCloud and viewable across a host of devices, such as an iPad or the iPhoto app on your Mac if you have one. This maxes out at 1,000 photos in 30 days. Once that limit is reached, older photos will be deleted. This, however, doesn't count towards your 5 GB iCloud storage.

Sharing Camera Roll Photos to Photo Stream

Once Photo Stream is enabled, you don't have to do anything to upload a photo. It's all done automatically, provided your iPhone is connected to Wi-Fi (if you're not, the iPhone will still upload the pictures next time you are).

Viewing the Photo Stream

Within the Albums section of the Photos app, there is a tab for Photo Stream. All of the photos you've shared to Photo Stream from your various Apple devices (not just those taken using the iPhone) are visible and sharable from this tab.

Viewing Photos from Other Apple Devices

Photo Stream – and indeed iCloud in general – is most useful to people who have multiple Apple devices. For example, if you have a Mac computer, photographs you

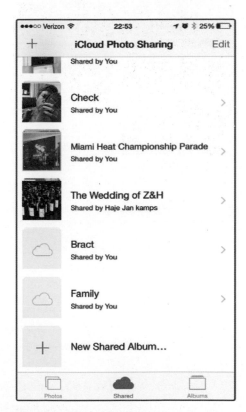

Hot Tip

Photo Stream stores up to 1,000 photos for 30 days so your recent pictures will always be available to you.

Above: My Photo Stream backs up your photos on iCloud.

Step 2: Select photos from your phone to add to a shared stream, which contacts can access and add to from their own Apple devices via iCloud.

import to the iPhoto program from your dedicated digital camera (Canon, Sony, etc.) can be automatically uploaded to Photo Stream (iPhoto > Preferences > Photo Stream > Automatic Upload) and will appear in your Photo Stream on the iPhone within seconds.

iCloud Photo Sharing

Although Photo Stream can be for personal use, you can also set up iCloud Photo Sharing to share photos and albums with others. Here's how to set up shared Photo Streams:

1. Go to Settings > Photos & Camera and switch on iCloud Photo Streams. Go to the Photos app.

2. Hit the Select button and tap the photos you'd like to share. Select the Share button and pick iCloud Photo Sharing.

3. A new sharing card will load with the photos attached. You can add a comment, select an existing shared album or create a new one.

Step 3: You can add comments before you add a photo to an iCloud shared album.

4. Browse to the Shared tab in the Photos app and select your new album. Then tap People > Invite People. Choose a contact and they'll be notified via email.

5. Choose whether subscribers can post as well. This is great if you would like the invited parties to share photos within this album too.

Family Albums

If you have Family Sharing set up, it'll automatically create an album within the Shared section of the Photos app. You can share pictures to this using the methods explained above.

EDITING AND SHARING VIDEOS

Videos shot on your iPhone can also be tweaked and sent out to the rest of the world – or just your mum.

Trim Video Recordings

The Trim tool dispenses with the unwanted portions of a video, making the clip nicer to look at and easier to share (due to the reduced file size).

Above: Edit video recordings using the Trim tool.

1. Select the video clip from the Camera Roll. There are markers at the beginning and end of each video. Drag the markers to where you'd like the clip to start and end.

Hot Tip
When uploading to social networks, use the Trim tool to keep it concise, thus making the upload quicker and easier.

Below: You can choose whether to publish a video to YouTube in Standard Definition or HD.

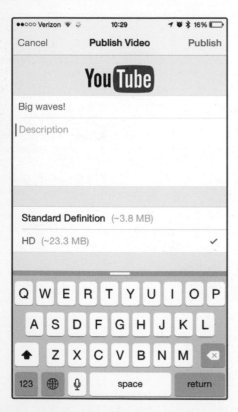

2.   The video timeline bar will turn yellow and a new Trim button will appear.

3.   Once the clip is tailored to your satisfaction, press the Play button to preview the new edit.

4.   Once you're happy, press Trim. You'll be asked whether you'd like to Trim Original or Save As New Clip; the latter will keep both versions. The new clip will then be ready to share.

Sharing Videos via Facebook, Email and Messages

To share a video, select the clip from the Camera Roll and hit the Share icon. You can select from the usual options Select Email or Messages to load the video in a blank email or message, add the contact details and accompanying text, and press Send.

Publish Videos to YouTube

Within the Share options for videos in the Camera Roll, you can also upload the video to YouTube, giving it a much larger potential audience. Here's how to do it:

1.   Select a video from the Camera Roll and hit Share.

2.   Select YouTube and type in your username and password. You can register for a free account at youtube.com, although Gmail users can use their Google login.

3. Type a title and description for the video in the respective fields.

4. Select Standard Definition or HD (Wi-Fi needed) quality.

5. Add tags and a category (optional) to make it more visible within YouTube searches.

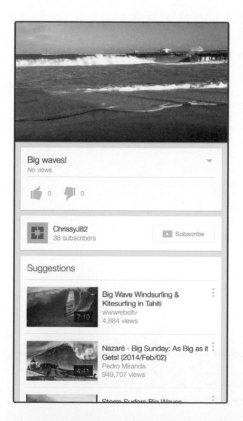

6. Make the video Public (available to anyone), Unlisted (available only to people with whom you share the link) or Private (only people you invite can view it). Select Publish.

7. Once the publishing process is complete, you'll see a Banner notification. You can View on YouTube or Tell a Friend (which launches a new email, complete with the YouTube link).

Left: Use your iPhone to view your video on YouTube.

MUSIC

The iPhone itself rose from the success of Apple's iPod. Hands up if you've owned an iPod? OK, everyone put your hands down now. The iPhone brings together the great audio quality and usability of an iPod, a music store and more.

GETTING MUSIC ON YOUR iPHONE

With the iTunes Store, your own existing music collection, music streaming apps such as Spotify and radio services like iHeartRadio, there is no limit to the level of aural satisfaction you can achieve using the iPhone.

Above: iTunes is a great digital library for your music. Select albums and tracks to transfer to your iPhone.

Downloading iTunes

The iTunes software for PC or Mac is the iPhone user's best friend. It acts as a home for your digital music library and lets you easily transfer it on to the iPhone. If you've ever owned a digital music player – such as the iPod – the chances are you've got a stack of digital music files just waiting to be transferred on to your iPhone. Here is how you download iTunes version 12 for Mac or PC:

1. Go to itunes.com and select Download.

2. On the next screen, add an email address, deselect the boxes (if you don't want junk email) and select Download Now.

3. Depending on which web browser you're using, you'll see an indicator of the download's progress. When the download is complete, select Open or locate the iTunes file in your computer's Downloads folder.

4. Follow the onscreen installation instructions.

Using an iTunes Account

In order to buy music, videos, apps, books or magazines from Apple's official portals, you'll need an Apple ID. Good thing we set one up in the first chapter isn't it? (If you did set up an Apple ID, you should be automatically signed in to the iTunes Store, and go to Step 2, below. If you didn't, go to Step 1, below).

1. Go to Settings > iCloud > Create a new Apple ID. Add your personal information, such as your name, date of birth, an email address and password, and choose three security questions and answers.

Step 1: When setting up your Apple ID, you will be asked to select security questions.

••ooo Verizon 🔋	10:53	🔋 📶 ≉ 29% 🔋⚡

Cancel   **Account Settings**

BILLING INFORMATION
You will not be charged until you make a purchase.

Visa

MasterCard

Amex

Discover

None   ✓

ITUNES GIFT CARDS AND ITUNES GIFTS

Code   Enter Code

BILLING ADDRESS

Title   Select a title

First Name   Chris

Back   Next

Step 3: You will be asked to enter payment details for your Apple ID in the iTunes Settings.

Hot Tip

If you have a large library and only want to sync certain artists to your iPhone, you can choose selected playlists, artists, albums and genres from the Sync music tab and apply each manually.

2. Head back to iTunes and the App Store in Settings and sign in.

3. As this is the first time it has been used, you'll be asked to set up a region and payment settings.

4. Once this is complete, you'll be able to start downloading music.

Transferring Music from iTunes

Now that you have iTunes installed on your laptop or desktop computer, you can plug in your iPhone and begin transferring all of that lovely digital music on to the device – here's how:

1. Plug your iPhone into your computer using the bundled-in charging cable. iTunes should load automatically and your iPhone will appear as a button in the top navigation menu in iTunes 12.

2. Click the iPhone icon and then Music in the side menu.

3. Select the Sync Music tick box. Pressing Sync to confirm will transfer your iTunes library on to the iPhone.

4. Next time you plug your iPhone into your computer, it will automatically sync your music to the phone, adding new songs and adjusting tweaked playlists.

iTunes Match

Got too much music to fit on the iPhone? Apple has a solution for you, through iCloud. iTunes Match subscribers have access to their entire music library on the go, without having to store it on the phone. The service scans your hard drive for all digital copies, matches them up with high-quality files from its store and lets you stream them over the internet. To subscribe for £22.99 a year, go to Settings > iTunes & App Store and then select Subscribe to iTunes Match.

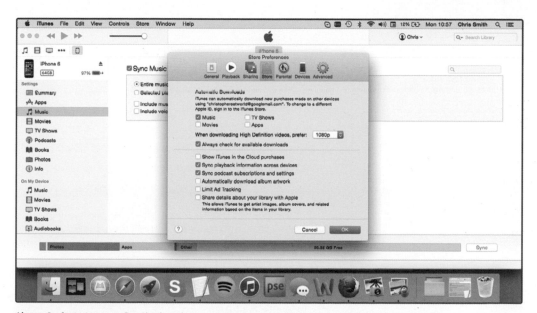

Above: Configure Automatic Downloads so that any items purchased on iTunes are downloaded straight to your iPhone.

iCloud Music

iCloud users can instantly re-download previously purchased music from iTunes on to their iPhone. Go to Settings > iTunes & App Store. Scroll down and enable Automatic Downloads for Music (and whatever else).

THE iTUNES MUSIC STORE

Thanks to the iTunes app that lives on your iPhone, you're able to download, play and own virtually any noteworthy song or album ever released. From the contemporary to the classic, it's all there waiting for you under one roof.

Buying Songs and Albums from iTunes

Hit the purple iTunes icon on your Home screen (it's not the red music app!) and, if it's the first time you've accessed the app, it will open with a splash page showcasing the store's new releases and featured artists.

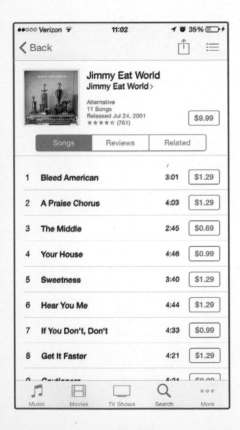

1. In order to search for specific songs, albums or artists, you can tap the Search tab at the foot of the screen.

2. Type the keywords of your choice (e.g. Mozart or Metallica) and hit Search.

3. The search will yield results applicable to your keywords, and you'll see a list of songs and albums. Next to each item, you'll see a button displaying the price. Tap this and select Buy.

4. Once you've entered your Apple ID password, the item will begin downloading and it will appear within the Music app (see page 192) when complete.

Previewing Songs

The iTunes app allows you to try before you buy. Just touch the name of a song and a 90-second preview will load and begin playing.

Left: View albums on iTunes to preview and purchase songs.

Chart Music

The iTunes Music Store also allows you to pick up the songs and albums currently topping the charts. Load the iTunes app and select Charts from the top menu to see the top songs, albums and music videos. Follow the instructions on the opposite page to buy this music.

FAMILY SHARING

Family Sharing is a new iCloud feature in iOS 8, which allows users to share music, apps, books and videos purchased by other members of the family. It also allows them to share their locations, schedule events on a family calendar and help each other find missing devices. It's also a great way to have one credit card on file and, if you have children, you can authorize all of their purchases. Here's how to set it up:

1. On your iPhone, go to iCloud within the Settings menu and select Set Up Family Sharing. Select Add Family Member.

2. Input the name or Apple ID email address of the family member and tap Next.

3. Select to send an email invitation or a passcode.

4. Once the family member has accepted the invitation, your accounts will be joined.

Any purchases they make will need to be authorised by the family 'organizer'. Purchases made, for example, from iTunes will be accessible from the Purchase section for each linked family member to download.

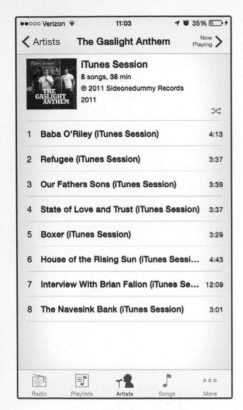

Above: Select an artist's name to view and play their albums and songs.

THE MUSIC APP

Now you have added your favourite music to the iPhone, you're ready to start playing it. The iPhone's Music app plays home to your new library. Open it and let's get started!

Choosing Music

Once you open the Music app, there are several different ways of accessing your music. The simplest is the Artists tab at the foot of the screen, which lists bands in alphabetical order, along with some artwork and information on how many albums/songs you have in your library.

The Now Playing Screen

When you select a song, album or playlist, what is currently playing will appear in a new screen, allowing you to control playback, volume, the next song and more. Here's a rundown of the media controls from within the Now Playing screen:

Right: The Now Playing screen gives you access to repeat, shuffle and other controls.

○ **Cover art**: album cover.

○ **Play/Pause**: Hit this icon to pause and restart playback.

○ **Previous/Next**: Move to the previous or next track on the list (hold these buttons to rewind or forward through an individual song).

Above: To browse your music using CoverFlow, flick one way or the other on the screen; flick fast to move through more covers, flick more slowly to move one at a time.

○ **Volume**: The bottom slider allows you to control the volume of a track. This will move up or down when you use the physical volume keys on the side of the device.

○ **Repeat**: Pressing this will allow you to select Repeat song or Repeat Artist.

○ **Create**: This option will create an iTunes Radio playlist from an artist or album. iTunes Radio is still awaiting a UK launch however, so be patient.

○ **Shuffle**: Tap Shuffle (two arrows intersecting with each other) to shuffle the current song queue (playlist, album, etc.).

○ **Song progress**: This slider shows you how much of the song has played and how much is left.

○ **Title bar**: Features the artist, song title and album.

○ **List view**: Select the List icon in the top-right corner to change the view and see the entire album or playlist.

○ **Back arrow**: Return to the previous screen.

Above: If the phone is unlocked, swipe up to the Control Center to quickly access music controls.

Multitasking with Music

Once you've selected your music, you're free to leave the app and send emails, browse the web or use most other apps without interrupting playback. You can return to the Music app to stop or change music but there are a couple of handy shortcuts to assist with this.

> ## Hot Tip
> Within the music app, at any time, turn the iPhone on its side to launch CoverFlow view, allowing you to flick through album covers and select them. Turning the phone back upright will revert to the previous view.

○ **While the phone is unlocked:** Swipe up from the bottom of the screen to reveal the Control Center. Here, you'll be able to Play, Pause, and access the Previous/Next control.

○ **While the phone is locked:** Tap the Home button. You'll see the cover art from the song you're currently playing and another set of media controls.

Creating Playlists

If you've synced your iTunes library by plugging your phone into your computer (*see* page 188), all of the playlists you've created in iTunes will be carried over to the iPhone too. You'll see them in the Playlists section of the Music app. However, from within the Playlists section of the Music app, you can also add new ones.

1. Select New Playlist, give it a name and press Save.

2. You'll now be asked to Add Songs. You can pick from existing folders like Playlists, Songs, Artists and Albums at the bottom of the screen. Tap the + icon to add songs.

3. Press Done when the playlist is complete.

4. Next time you plug your phone into iTunes, the Playlist will sync back to iTunes too.

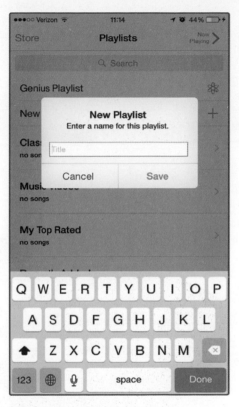

Step 1: Enter a name and touch Save; you can then begin adding songs to your new playlist.

Other Music Services

Although iTunes is a one-stop shop for your music needs, there's a world of fantastic music services out there. Turn to page 250 to see a list of our favourites.

SHARING MUSIC TO SPEAKERS

If you're at home, you can play music through the iPhone's speakers; they're actually not bad on the iPhone 6 and can reach a decent decibel level. If you're in public, you can use any set of headphones with a 3.5-mm jack. However, if you're looking to crank up the volume, you can have your music super loud with the aid of a speaker.

Speaker Docks

Made popular in the iPod era, speaker docks allow you to plug your iPhone into a connector in order to play music through a more powerful set of speakers. Some speaker docks are great, because they'll also charge your iPhone while it is docked.

Above: Some AirPlay speakers allow you to listen to music and charge your phone at the same time.

AirPlay Speakers

AirPlay is a wireless technology developed by Apple to share music and video over Wi-Fi networks. If you have AirPlay-enabled speakers (they're available from Bose, B&W, Sony, JBL, Philips and more), you can send any music from your iPhone to the speakers without plugging in. If an AirPlay speaker is connected to the same Wi-Fi network as your iPhone, you'll see the AirPlay icon in Command Center (swipe up from the bottom of the screen). Tap AirPlay and select the speaker.

Hot Tip

If you own an Apple TV set-top box, you can send music directly to your TV set.

Bluetooth Speakers

You can also use the iPhone's Bluetooth connectivity to connect to speakers – here's how:

1. Make sure that Bluetooth is enabled on the device you'd like to pair with.

2. Enter the iPhone Settings and select Bluetooth. Toggle the switch to turn Bluetooth on.

3. The iPhone will go into Discovery mode and search for speakers with Bluetooth connectivity.

4. When you find your speakers (usually under the manufacturer's name and model number), select them.

5. You may be asked for a four-digit PIN code to connect to the speaker (see your instruction manual). Once the initial connection is made, it will connect automatically in future.

6. Enter the Music app (or Spotify or internet radio apps, etc.) and start playing.

Wired Speakers

You can also connect speakers through the iPhone's headphone jack.

VIDEO

The iPhone is a staggeringly powerful tool for video. Not only can it record video in full high-definition, but you can also play your favourite TV shows and movies, stream them from the internet and purchase brand new films to rent and own. If you've got an iPhone 6 Plus, you can now view video in stunning 1080p high definition.

ADDING VIDEO CONTENT TO YOUR iPHONE

If you read the section in this chapter on syncing your music files, then you'll soon notice that the process of getting video content on to your phone is pretty similar. It can be bought or streamed directly from the internet, or added from your existing library.

Above: Sync your favorite TV shows over iTunes so that you can watch them on your iPhone.

Syncing Video via iTunes

Just as we did with music, it's possible to transfer existing videos you may have previously purchased or added to iTunes directly on to your iPhone.

1. Plug your iPhone into your computer using the USB cable; iTunes should automatically load (if you don't have iTunes, *see* page 187).

2. Select the iPhone from the navigation menu.

3. From the content menu on the left-hand side, select Movies or TV Shows. You'll see a list of videos you currently have within your iTunes library.

4. Tick Sync Movies/TV Shows and then begin selecting the content you'd like to add.

5. Alternatively, tick the Automatically Include box and select from the drop-down menu to set rules (all movies, most recent, unwatched, etc).

6. The Capacity bar at the bottom of the iTunes screen will tell you how much space you have on the device and will update as you add video files.

7. When you're done, press Sync and the movies or TV shows will begin to load on to your device. Don't unplug the iPhone until this process is complete.

iPhone/iTunes Video Formats

Apple likes to keep things tidy, but it also likes you to buy things from them. To that end, it limits the video formats that work in iTunes and on the iPhone. The files need to be .MPEG-4 or .H.264 to play on the device. Videos in other popular formats, such as .WMV and .AVI, will not work on the iPhone or in iTunes.

Hot Tip

It is possible to watch videos in formats not recognized by Apple, such as .WMV or .AVI; they can be converted on your computer using software such as Handbreak (www.handbreak.com).

BUYING FROM THE iTUNES STORE

As is the case with music, you can purchase a world of movie and TV content through the iTunes app on your iPhone.

Finding Video Content

Open the iTunes app and select the Movies or TV Shows tab to see featured content. This will show new releases and recently aired shows. In order to locate content, hit the Search button and type in the title of your choice.

Above: The video product page gives added info about movies or TV shows featured on iTunes.

The Video Product Page

Once you've found the movie of your choice, you'll be taken to its product page, where you'll have the opportunity to view trailers. You'll also see a plot summary, cast and crew list, and a certificate, and you'll get the chance to read reviews from other users.

Buying to Own

Buying video content from the iTunes app means that the digital file is yours to keep for ever. You can transfer it to as many Apple devices as you please and it will always be associated with your Apple ID if you want to re-download it.

1. Identify the movie or TV show you wish to own. Click the Buy button and enter your account password. Once that's entered, the file will start downloading.

2. You can see its progress by selecting More > Downloads within iTunes and it'll give you an indication of how long is left to download.

3. In order to start watching as the movie is downloading, exit iTunes and enter the Video app. It'll be waiting for you.

4. Select the title to begin playback.

Renting Movies

iTunes movie rentals are perfect if you just want to watch a movie once rather than have it to own. The price is around the same as renting a DVD from your local video store (remember those?). In iTunes, you follow the same procedure as buying a movie (unfortunately, TV shows can only be bought to own), except that you hit the Rent button from the product page.

There are a couple of caveats with renting movies though. Once you begin to watch the film, it has to be finished within 24 hours. Otherwise, you have 30 days before the rental expires. The Video app will tell you how long you have left to view the video.

HD or SD?

Prices for movies and TV shows are automatically displayed for the HD version but, if you're not concerned about the highest quality, you get the video more cheaply by scrolling to the bottom of the product page screen and selecting Also Available in SD (Standard Definition).

Hot Tip

Be patient! Movie files can be around 3 GB in size, so they will take a while to download completely. Movies can only be downloaded over Wi-Fi.

Above: The Video app tells you how long you have left to view a rented iTunes movie.

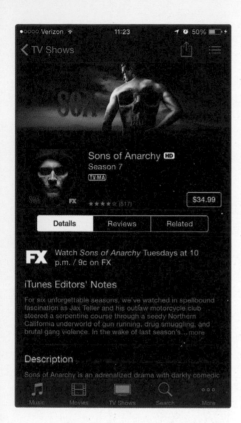

Above: For TV series, you can either buy a pass to view the whole season or scroll down to select a certain episode.

Season Pass or Episodes?

If you're buying TV shows from iTunes, you'll have the option to pick up the latest episode or to buy a pass, which gives you the entire season. The first option is great if you have a favourite episode or you missed one when it was aired on TV. The season home page will point you towards buying the whole season, but scroll down the page to access particular episodes.

iCloud Movies

Above: You can download previous movie purchases to your phone by connecting to Wi-Fi and using iCloud.

Since movie and TV show files are so large, you may not be able to fit multiple films on the iPhone at one time – especially if you've only got the 16-GB model.

iTunes in the iCloud keeps a record of everything you've bought from the store (either from the iTunes computer app for Mac and PC, or on your iPhone or iPad) and lets you reacquire the content wirelessly. To re-download previous purchases, go to iTunes > More > Purchased and select the iCloud download button from the title page. The file will then be downloaded to your device.

THE VIDEO APP

The iPhone's Video app houses all of the content you currently have stored on the device, either transferred from iTunes or bought/rented from iTunes, as explained in previous sections. Everything appears in list format, under Movies and TV Shows. Items saved in the cloud can be streamed to the device rather than downloaded.

Playing Movies

The video playback screen on the iPhone is a lot simpler than the music equivalent. Selecting a video from the app will instantly start playback.

iTunes Sharing Over Wi-Fi

If your iPhone and computer are connected to the same mobile network,

Above: Playing movies in the Video app is simple. When you touch the screen, it will display Play, Pause, Rewind and Forward buttons, along with a progress bar.

you can stream items from your iTunes library directly to your iPhone. Open the Video app and select Shared. Select your Library and all of the video files listed on your computer will show up; you can then play them as normal.

AirPlay via Apple TV

When you're watching a movie on the train on the way home from work, wouldn't it be nice to just send it to your television when you get through the door and relax in your favourite chair to watch the ending? If you have an Apple TV set-top box, that's exactly what you can do.

We mentioned AirPlay in the Music section, but it extends to video for Apple TV owners too. Videos from an increasing number of apps and websites now have AirPlay support. Here's how to share video with your TV:

1. You'll need to be registered on the same Wi-Fi network as the Apple TV.

2. If It's in range, you'll see the AirPlay icon in the video playback controls. Tap this and select Apple TV.

Hot Tip

If you exit the Video app at any time, the next time you open it, the last video you were watching can be resumed from where you left off.

3. The video will automatically be transferred at exactly the same point in your viewing.

Above: Selecting the AirPlay icon in the Command Center allows you to use AirPlay to transfer content to your Apple TV at home.

VIDEO STREAMING SERVICES

Although Apple would love you to rent and buy videos only from the iTunes Store, there are plenty of other alternatives in the App Store for streaming video over the internet. Here are some of our favourites; see also a list of our favourite apps on page 251.

- **Amazon Prime Instant Video**: Formerly LoveFilm, subscribers can access thousands of movies and TV shows through the iPhone app (amazon.co.uk).

- **Netflix**: Watch movies and TV on your iPhone for a monthly fee (netflix.com).

- **YouTube**: There's a dedicated YouTube iPhone app available from the App Store, featuring billions of user-uploaded videos.

- **BBC iPlayer**: The iPlayer app allows users to get free access to recent (and selected older) BBC TV shows. Programming can be downloaded over Wi-Fi and watched offline.

- **Sky Go**: This allows live streaming of a host of channels (including Sky Sports, Sky Movies and Sky One) over Wi-Fi and 3G (you need to subscribe to Sky TV).

- **Wuaki.tv**: Use this app to watch your favourite TV series and also rent or buy movies, in both HD and SD.

Above: The Netflix app allows you to stream thousands of movies and TV shows.

READING

If you have an iPhone, you'll never be short of something to read – that's a promise. From brand-new bestsellers to the classic books of yesteryear, the iBooks store is your oyster, while Newsstand provides instant access to many popular magazines.

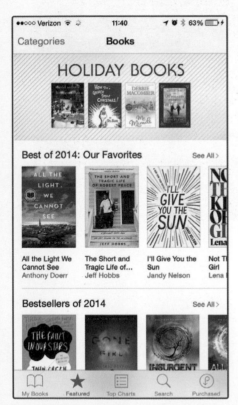

Above: Search the iBooks store for free and paid books available for instant download.

BOOKS

Apple's digital bookstore, built into your iPhone, is called iBooks. Selecting this app will load a bookshelf, which you'll find is currently empty. However, there are several other tabs at the foot of the screen that allow you to purchase and download books.

- **Featured**: Just like the App Store, the iBooks Store offers a selection of featured content. It could be categories like 'Books Made into Movies' or 'Christmas Books,' etc.

- **Top Charts**: Touching this tab will display the most popular books in the store. You'll be able to choose between books, the *New York Times* bestseller list and Top Authors. Select an author from the list to load their titles. You can also pick Paid and Free books.

- **Search**: The easiest way to find a specific book is through the Search tab. Simply type the name of the book or the author to load the relevant titles.

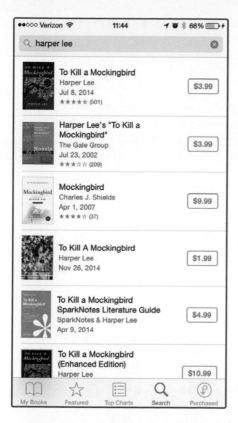

Above: You can search for a book by typing an author's name or book title into the search bar.

○ **Purchased:** This will show your previously purchased books, allowing you to download them to your shelf if they're not there already.

Buying a Book from iBooks

Once you've identified the book of your choice, you can buy it from the product page. Tap the Buy Book button, enter your Apple ID password and the book will be downloaded. It will then appear on your bookshelf.

Book Samples

When browsing in a bricks and mortar bookshop, it's only natural to flick through a few pages before paying. The iBook store has an equivalent through the Sample feature.

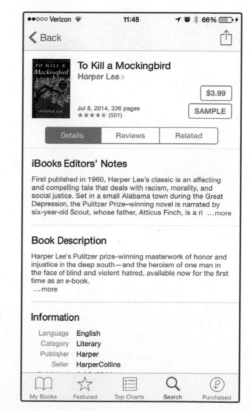

On the product page, you can hit Sample and a few pages will be downloaded to your virtual bookshelf. Many books even let you read the entire first chapter before committing to buying.

Right: When you select a book, you will be presented with the blue purchase option. Touch this button and enter your Apple ID to pay for the book and download it to your bookshelf.

Above: There are many free books available to download to your shelf.

Free Books

Publishing laws mean that once a published book has been around for a certain amount of time, copyright expires and it becomes freely available. You can download free books from the likes of Charles Dickens, Jane Austen, Mark Twain, William Shakespeare and more.

iCloud and iBooks

Apple's iCloud means that all previous purchases are available to read on your iPhone too. The Purchased tab lists the books that you have bought through iTunes on your computer or through the iBooks app on the iPad. Hit the Cloud icon to the right of the book to add these titles to your iPhone's bookshelf.

Hot Tip

Tap the Categories button to narrow down the charts based on genres (biography, romance, etc.).

READING iBOOKS

Now you have stocked your virtual bookshelf with a host of titles from the iBooks Store, it's time to start reading. Select the thumbnail cover from the Library to load the book full-screen on your device.

Turning Pages

The pages in iBooks turn as if you were reading a real book and it's one of the best-looking things you can do on an iPhone. Use your thumb to slowly drag from various points on the right side of the page to see this beautifully imagined feature in all its glory. You can also give the screen a little flick when you're ready to turn a page. Naturally, when going back a page, flick from left to right.

Finding a Page

If you're searching for a particular page within a book, there are a number of ways to reach it quickly:

- **Contents:** Tap the list icon at the top of the screen, where you can access the Contents page. Tap an item from the page to head to the beginning of that chapter.

- **Scan:** At the foot of the screen, you'll see a bar. Drag this back and forth to find specific pages. Take your finger off the screen when you've reached the page you want.

- **Search:** Hit the Search icon at the top of the screen and type in words or a page number. Make your selection from the list of results.

Hot Tip

If you ever get bored of the page-turning mechanism (we haven't), you can just tap the screen to turn a page.

●●○○○ Verizon 🖥	11:54	⬆ 🔋 73% 🔋⚡

Library Resume **Different Seasons** ⬆

Contents	Bookmarks	Notes

Title Page	13
Copyright Page	15
Dedication	17
Praise	18
HOPE SPRINGS ETERNAL	19
Rita Hayworth and Shawshank Redemption	20
SUMMER OF CORRUPTION	166
Apt Pupil	167
FALL FROM INNOCENCE	450
The Body	451

Above: Touch the List icon at the top of your screen to display the book's contents page.

- **Bookmarks**: You can add as many Bookmarks as you wish by pressing the icon at the top of the screen. All Bookmarks can be accessed by tapping the List icon and selecting the Bookmarks tab.

Changing the View

iBooks enables you to tailor your reading experience. Tap the small and large A icon to load the options, as follows:

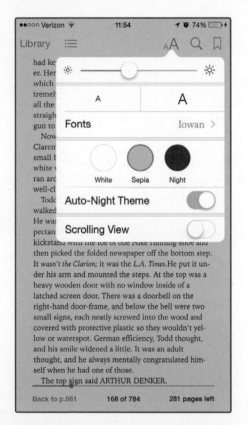

Above: Touch the A icon to alter viewing options such as brightness and theme.

- **Brightness**: Rather than exiting the app to change the brightness, you can do it directly from the iBooks app.

- **Text size**: Hit the 'A' buttons to increase or decrease the size of the text.

- **Fonts**: iBooks boasts seven fonts. Pick your favourite from the list.

- **Themes**: Choose your desired colour scheme: black text on a white background, brown text on a sepia background or light grey text on a black background.

- **Auto Night** Enabling this option will automatically convert the theme to white on black.

- **Scrolling View**: Turning on Scrolling View will allow you to read the book on a continuous page, rather than having to turn each page.

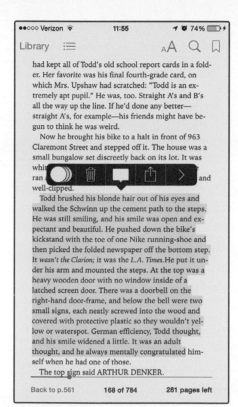

Above: You can select text sections to copy, define or highlight.

Above: You can paste highlighted sections into Notes.

Adding Highlights, Copying Text and Making Notes

iBooks also allows users to annotate the text with notes and highlights, while sections can also be copied and shared. In order to use these features, you'll need to select a piece of text. Hold the screen and move the two blue markers to highlight the relevant section of the text. You'll see an Options tab pop up, allowing you to do the following:

○ **Copy:** This will copy a segment of the text, allowing you to paste it into another app (e.g. email, document, etc.).

○ **Define:** If you've highlighted a particular word, you can ask iBooks for a dictionary definition.

○ **Highlight:** Tapping Highlight will turn the section yellow, but it will also bring up a new Options screen, allowing you to change the colour, delete the highlight, share it or add a note.

○ **Note:** This allows you to annotate text. The selected text will open in a new window. Type your notes and press Done to return to the page. To edit what you have written, tap the Post-it note next to the section.

Search: Tapping Search will give you the option of searching for the passage elsewhere on your phone, or via the web (Google) or Wikipedia.

Share: Share a favourite passage via the usual means.

KINDLE

Many people who graduate to using an iPhone own or have owned an Amazon Kindle ebook reader and are likely to have a library of digital books they've already bought. Thankfully, there's a Kindle app for the iPhone, where users can access all of their previous purchases.

The Kindle App

This application can be downloaded for free from the App Store (see page 160). Once you have opened it, enter your Amazon username and password, and select Register this Kindle. All of your previous purchases will be listed, so tap the cover to download each item. You can't buy books from the Kindle app; instead, you'll need to do that from amazon.com. Fret not though: after purchase, the books will still appear in the iPhone app.

Reading a Kindle Book

Kindle Books can take advantage of Amazon's neat Whispersync technology, which means whenever you open a book in the Kindle app, it will sync to the last page you read on any of your devices. Beyond that, the means of reading books doesn't differ much from iBooks.

> ## Hot Tip
> Briefly holding your finger down on the screen and dragging downwards will highlight that section of text.

Above: Enter your Amazon username and password and tap Register this Kindle to begin using the free app.

MAGAZINES AND NEWSPAPERS

Beyond books, you can also have many high-profile periodicals delivered straight to your iPhone. This is done through the Newsstand app on the iPhone's Home screen.

Newsstand

If you've used the iTunes Store for buying music and movies, Newsstand will feel very familiar. Hitting the Store button within the app will take you to the featured content. You can browse New & Noteworthy and the All Newsstand Titles sections or use the Search tab to look for something specific. Once you've found a title you like, hit the thumbnail image to download it to your Newsstand.

Downloading Issues and Subscribing

Adding a magazine to your Newsstand app won't give you immediate access to any content – just the opportunity to subscribe for a particular period of time or download individual issues from within the app. Select the option of your choice by clicking the price. All purchases will be charged back to your iTunes account, just like music and movies.

Below: Browse the Newsstand list to look for publications to download.

Hot Tip

When a new issue is available to download, you'll receive a notification from Newsstand and a number will appear next to the cover.

Above: The Guardian app is a free newspaper app designed for mobiles.

NEWSPAPERS

As with magazines, the leading UK newspapers are yet to embrace Newsstand on the iPhone, because it's difficult to format a full newspaper on such a small screen. However, all British dailies have dedicated apps available from the App Store. Some offer free access, whereas others will make you pay to subscribe.

Free Newspaper Apps

The *Guardian*, *Daily Mirror*, *Daily Mail*, *Daily Express*, the *Independent* and *Daily Star* all offer free apps that you can download from the App Store. These are, essentially, mobile-optimized versions of their websites, which can also be accessed over the web through Safari.

Subscription Newspaper Apps

Some newspapers make you pay to access their content through the iPhone app. *The Daily Telegraph* (£9.99 a month), *The Times* (£9.99 a month) and *The Sun* (69p for the app download and then 69p per month) all have a paywall. Users can subscribe to the newspaper from within the app, which will be charged to their Apple ID and will auto-renew each month.

Other News Applications

Beyond the traditional daily newspapers, there are other ways to obtain your news through stand-alone apps on the iPhone. The BBC News app offers a brilliant design with written, audio and video content, while Sky News and Channel 4 News bring great video content from their broadcasts. All three can be downloaded from the App Store.

Hot Tip

To stop auto-renewals, open iTunes on your computer, select your account page and scroll to Subscriptions, then tap Manage.

GAMING

All iPhone games are available to download from within the App Store and can be obtained using the methods explained in the previous chapter on apps.

PLAYING GAMES ON A TOUCH SCREEN

The multi-touch screen on the iPhone makes it a powerful gaming device. It means you can perform a host of swiping, tapping, zooming, pinching, dragging and flicking gestures using more than one digit at a time. The entire screen is your control pad and it helps to give each game its own unique flavour, while breathing new life into classic titles from yesteryear.

We'll use a few of the App Store's most popular games as examples, to help you get started and to explain the different ways to control games using the phone. See also the list of our favourites on page 252.

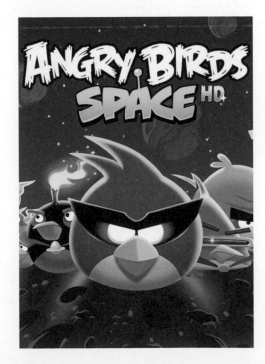

- **Line up and launch (e.g. Angry Birds):** Once you've downloaded the game from the App Store (there are free and paid versions), it's easy to get started. Pull back the slingshot to aim the Angry Birds at the pigs and then release it to fire. You'll need to get the angle and the power right to hit your target.

- **Swipe and slash (e.g. Fruit Ninja):** Use your thumb or finger as a sword to slash the falling fruits in two. Once you get the hang of Fruit Ninja, try Infinity Blade, where you need to use a sword against a host of beasties from another world.

Above: Scrabble has been redesigned for the iPhone. Play by dragging and dropping letters.

○ **Drag and drop (e.g. Scrabble):** One of our favourite classic board games that has been reinvented for the iPhone is Scrabble. You pick a letter and drag-and-drop it on to the board to form words, and the game will do the rest.

○ **Virtual buttons (e.g. FIFA Soccer):** Scaled-down versions of Xbox 360 and PlayStation 4 games feature virtual buttons and directional arrows, which allow you to pass, shoot, tackle and move players, in lieu of the traditional gaming pad.

○ **Tilting and turning (e.g. Asphalt 8):** Racing games are amazing on the iPhone. With the gyroscopic sensor and built-in accelerometer, you can tilt the phone to steer the car left and right. Platform games like Temple Run are also brilliant for using this method.

GAME CENTER

The Game Center app on your iPhone's Home screen allows you to challenge friends to games online, while it also keeps track of your personal accomplishments on each game you play. When you first load the app, you'll need to sign in with your Apple ID and password.

Achievements and Leaderboards

Each game you play on your iOS device will be listed in Game Center. If applicable, you'll see your worldwide ranking, global leaderboards and the achievements you've unlocked within each game.

Hot Tip

When you first log into Game Center, allow the app to search your Facebook friends for those already using the app.

Above: The Game Center app displays your games and leaderboards.

Adding Friends in Game Center

Once you've added your iPhone-toting friends to your Game Center account, you can view the games they're playing and challenge them to multiplayer battles. Alternatively, you can hit the + button to add friends individually from your Contacts book.

Multiplayer Games

Many games allow for multiple participants. Some games, like Scrabble, have their own mechanisms for finding online opponents; Game Center also helps to pair you up with partners or adversaries over Wi-Fi.

Above: You can challenge friends to unlock Achievements in games and beat your own scores.

Challenge Friends

You can try to beat your friends' high scores by finding them in Game Center. Challenges you receive will appear in the Challenges tab, and you can also browse your friends and select their achievements and scores.

ADVANCED iPHONE

CUSTOMIZING

The ability to personalize your handset, customizing how it looks and behaves, is one of the biggest draws of the iPhone. Like a made-to-measure suit, you can refine almost everything the iPhone does so that it feels like it's designed to accommodate all your habits and idiosyncrasies.

SETTINGS

To customize tools and apps, choose Settings from your Home screen. Here, you'll see a list of everything you can amend, from Wi-Fi and Sounds, to Privacy, Apps, Camera and more. Just click on the small > next to each item to dig deeper into its settings. You can access many of these settings just by swiping up from the foot of the screen to access the Control Center.

PREFERENCES

Airplane Mode

Using your mobile to make calls in-flight is not possible or allowed, but once you hit cruising altitude, you may want to listen to music, watch a film or play a game. In Settings, just toggle Airplane Mode on before you take off. This shuts down the phone's wireless functions, including Wi-Fi, 3G, Bluetooth and 4G. A small Airplane icon will appear in the status bar to show you it's activated.

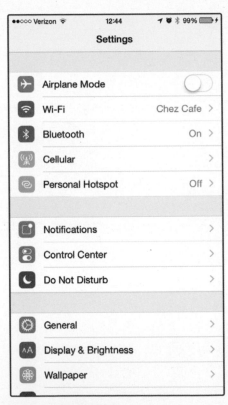

Above: The Settings page allows you to amend and customize many features.

Bluetooth Preferences

Bluetooth lets your iPhone communicate wirelessly with other devices such as headsets, fitness trackers, speakers or phones. You can switch it on and off in Control Center. However, in order to manage your Bluetooth setup, go to Settings and select Bluetooth. Here, you'll see a list of nearby devices. When Bluetooth is on, a small symbol appears in the status bar. When the Bluetooth icon turns white (rather than grey), it is connected to another device.

Managing which devices your iPhone can communicate with is simple:

○ **To connect or disconnect a device**: Tap the name until the words Connected or Not Connected appear.

○ **To unpair a device**: Tap the blue 'i', select Forget This Device and it will no longer appear in your list of available devices.

CONTINUITY

Continuity is another iOS 8 feature that will come into its own (Health is another) in the future, rather than right now, so we haven't gone into detail until this section. The idea is to improve the way iPhones work with Mac computers and iPad tablets. Here are some examples of how Continuity can work. It's quite complex in terms of system requirements for each element, and large numbers of you won't yet be able to access any of them.

Hot Tip
Ignored a Bluetooth device by mistake? Turn off your iPhone. When you reboot, the Bluetooth device you previously ignored will be back on the list.

Above: Turning your Bluetooth on causes a small icon to appear in the status bar.

iPhone Cellular Calls

When you receive a phone call on your iPhone, you'll be able to answer it on a Mac or an iPad with Continuity. You'll also be able to start calls from those devices if it's more convenient. This works with any iPhone/iPad on iOS 8 and up and any Mac with Mac OS X Yosemite and up.

SMS Relay

With Continuity enabled, when you get a text message from a non-iPhone device (say, an Android phone), that will also appear in your Messages app on Mac and iPad. This allows you to reply using the device closest to you. Conversations can be started using the means listed above for phone calls.

Above: If you have a recent Mac as well as an iPhone, you'll be able to receive regular SMS messages on it.

Instant Hotspot

If you're out of Wi-Fi range, you can share your iPhone's mobile data connection with your Mac or iPad using Continuity's Instant Hotspot feature. If you have the right gear running the right software, the iPhone's connection should automatically be available in the Wi-Fi menus on the iPad and Mac, allowing you to easily connect. If you don't have the tech necessary, you can still share your internet connection using Personal Hotspot (*see* page 228).

Above: If you're out of Wi-Fi range your iPad or Mac can connect to your iPhone's Personal Hotspot.

Handoff

With Handoff, you can start a task on one device and finish it on another. Within the context of Mail, that means you can start composing an email on one device and complete it on another when your handset is in Bluetooth range. It's not just Mail; it also works with

Safari, Maps, Messages, Reminders, Calendar, Contacts, Pages, Numbers, and Keynote. System requirements are the same as Instant Hotspot listed above.

AirDrop

Another part of Continuity is AirDrop, a sharing technology that's available to some iPhone users. It can be used to exchange files with other iPhones, iPads (fourth generation or later) and newer Mac computers (running OS X Yosemite) in the near vicinity.

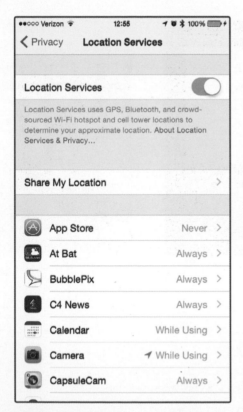

Above: You can choose which apps are allowed to access your whereabouts in Location Services.

PRIVACY PREFERENCES

Your iPhone uses two methods to pinpoint where you are: built-in sat nav-style GPS (Global Positioning System) or by triangulating signals from mobile phone masts and Wi-Fi points. These slightly sci-fi capabilities are used for everything, from helping you to navigate while using the Maps app to tagging photos you've taken with a location. If you feel that this is all a bit more Big Brother than you're happy with, you can go 'off the grid'. Individual apps should ask your permission to use Location Services via pop-up messages, but you can also turn off Location Services completely by going to Settings > Privacy and toggling to Off.

More Location Preferences

You'll find a System Services button at the bottom of the Location Settings screen. Tap this and you'll be given the option to turn off several settings that relate to your phone network, location-based iAds and time zone.

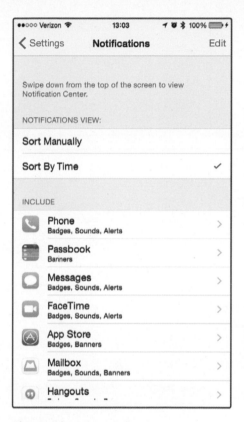

Above: Notification settings allow you to alter alerts for individual apps.

Notifications Settings

iPhone Notifications provide a variety of different ways to alert you when something is received, updated or you've set a reminder. In addition to showing up as Alerts, Banners and Sounds, these updates also appear in the Notifications Center, which is accessed by swiping down from the top of the Home screen. You can fine-tune how and when your alerts appear in Notifications Settings.

○ **To assign Notifications Settings for an app:**
   Go to Settings > Notifications and select the app from the list. You can then toggle the Sounds, Alerts, Banners and Badges to On or Off for that app, as well as deciding whether the alerts appear in the main Notification Center.

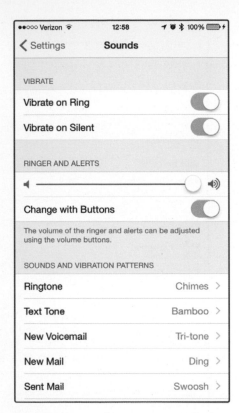

Above: Sound settings allow you to customize all audio aspects of your iPhone.

Hot Tip

To make your battery last longer, switch on the Auto-Brightness function in Settings > Display & Brightness and the iPhone will adjust itself, depending on light conditions.

Sound Settings

Go to Settings > Sounds. From here, you can switch audio alerts on or off, for everything from incoming email through to calendar alerts. You can also assign each function its own tone, manage your ringtones, set volume levels and decide whether or not your phone should vibrate when you have an alert.

GENERAL SETTINGS

Many of the features we've discussed in this book can be altered in the Settings > General section. Here, you'll find information about software updates, Siri, Usage, Auto-Lock, iTunes Wi-Fi Sync and more.

About Your Phone

Want to know how many songs, videos, photos and apps are on your phone? Or how much space you have left to store more content? You need to check out the About section in Settings > General, which is where all the nitty-gritty but important details about your phone live. Other things you'll find lurking here include: software version (e.g. iOS 8), model and serial numbers, Wi-Fi address and network information.

Software Update

Head here to find out if there's a software update for your phone. See page 44 for information on how to update your phone.

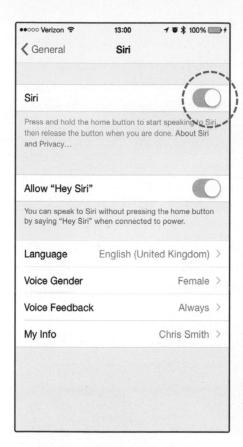

Above: Siri settings include language and voice-feedback options.

Siri

Here, you can choose the language Siri speaks, decide whether you always want voice feedback, and teach it more about you by providing personal information under My Info. This will allow you to say, for example, 'Siri, take me home' to load directions in Maps.

'Hey Siri'

A new feature in iOS 8 is the ability to access Siri without holding down the Home button. If you enable this in Settings, you'll be able to say 'Hey Siri' to summon the app. This only works when the phone is plugged into a power source.

Below: Remember to switch off Data Roaming when travelling abroad to save costly charges outside of your price plan.

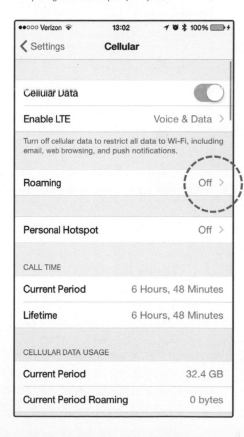

Data Roaming

If you're heading abroad and you haven't got a data plan with built-in allowances, then using your phone for data-heavy activities (surfing the web, checking your Facebook app or sending emails) can prove costly. Go into Settings > Celluar > Data Roaming and toggle to Off.

●●○○○ Verizon LTE 13:05 ⌖ ◉ ✳ 100% ▭✦

‹ Settings **Personal Hotspot**

Personal Hotspot

Now Discoverable.
Other users can look for your shared network using Wi-Fi
and Bluetooth under the name "iPhone 6".

Wi-Fi Password zz7m6qag1o4bb ›

TO CONNECT USING WI-FI
1 Choose "iPhone 6" from the Wi-Fi settings on
   your computer or other device.
2 Enter the password when prompted.

TO CONNECT USING BLUETOOTH
1 Pair iPhone with your computer.
2 On iPhone, tap Pair or enter the code displayed
   on your computer.
3 Connect to iPhone from computer.

TO CONNECT USING USB
1 Plug iPhone into your computer.
2 Choose iPhone from the list of network services
   in your settings.

Above: If your network provider allows it, you can
enable Personal Hotspot to share your data connection
with other devices.

iTunes Wi-Fi Sync

You can sync your iPhone to a PC or
Mac without needing to physically
connect the device with a USB cable. If
Wi-Fi syncing has been set up in iTunes
(see page 41 for syncing via iTunes), a
Sync Now button will appear. Hit this and
your devices will do their thing.

Personal Hotspot

If you're in a no-Wi-Fi zone, you can share the
iPhone's internet connection with a computer,
iPhone or iPad, provided your network allows it (or
you pay extra for the privilege!). To enable this, go
into Settings and select Personal Hotspot and
toggle the button on or off as required. This will
see the iPhone show up as a Wi-Fi network for
other devices. To connect, you can give them the
password generated within Personal Hotspot.

Customizing Your Keyboard

You can change the way your iPhone keyboard works; go into Settings > General > Keyboard. There, you can enable many special functions, such as Auto-Capitalization, Enable Caps Lock and Auto Correction. You can also add an international keyboard.

New Keyboards

Apple iOS 8 introduces the ability to switch the standard iPhone keyboard for others from the App Store. This means you can use keyboards like Swype, that enable you to swipe between letters to form words, or SwiftKey that learns from your writing patterns. Once you've downloaded it, you will need to go to Settings > General > Keyboard > Add New Keyboard and select the Third-Party Keyboard from the list to install it. When typing a message or email, select the Globe icon to switch between the keyboards.

Reset Settings

Only the brave, the desperate or the foolish mess around with the Reset settings (Settings > General > Reset). Luckily, you'll need a password before you can hit the big red buttons, but here's what each of them does, should you decide to proceed:

- **Reset all settings**: Resets your settings to default, but does not affect your data or media.

Above: New keyboards like SwiftKey are available in iOS 8.

Hot Tip

Create your own keyboard short cuts to make typing faster. Go into Settings > Keyboard and Add Shortcuts. You'll be able to type things like 'GTBL' and the full text 'Going to be late' will appear as a suggestion as you type.

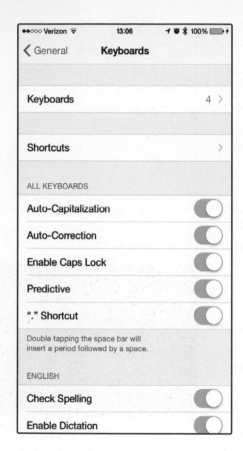

Above: After entering a password, you are able to begin resetting your phone settings.

○ **Erase All Content and Settings**: Deletes all data and resets the settings to default.

○ **Reset Network Settings**: Restores your phone's network settings to the factory defaults.

○ **Reset Keyboard Dictionary**: Removes any words you may have added to the dictionary.

○ **Reset Home Screen Layout**: Makes your Home screen factory fresh.

○ **Reset Location & Privacy**: Restores default settings for location and privacy.

Twitter

In Settings > General, hitting the Twitter button lets you add a new account. If you select Update, it will scan your contacts, adding Twitter handles and photos where available. You can select which apps you want to use with Twitter.

Facebook

Within Facebook settings, you can turn on Calendar and Contacts settings. This will add details of your Facebook pals to your phone contacts and it will also drop their birthdays into your iPhone Calendar. Remember that the iPhone will try to match Facebook contacts with contacts already in your address book (for more details on managing Facebook contacts on your iPhone, *see* page 112).

TROUBLESHOOTING

Even good gadgets go wrong, and the iPhone isn't immune to the odd glitch. This section will help you to overcome most of the problems you're likely to encounter.

CONNECTIVITY

Bugs are often fixed by iOS updates, but if you can't wait for new software, there are techy solutions on the web – be warned though: these tend to be complicated. So before you start meddling with DNS settings, here are some simple cures to most connection quibbles.

Wireless

Here are some checks to run through if you're having problems connecting to the Wi-Fi:

- **Is Wi-Fi enabled?** Tap Settings > Wi-Fi and make sure that Wi-Fi is turned on.

- **Connected to a network?** No? Pick an available Wi-Fi network from the list you'll find under Choose a Network and tap the one you want to join.

- **Entered a password?** Double-check that your password is correct.

- **Check the signal:** The Wi-Fi icon in the status bar shows a varying number of bars to indicate the signal strength. More bars equal a stronger signal.

Above: If you are having connectivity problems, check your Wi-Fi settings.

Hot Tip

On public networks, your browser will often redirect you to a login page. Until you've signed in, the status bar will show you're connected, but you won't be able to use the Wi-Fi network.

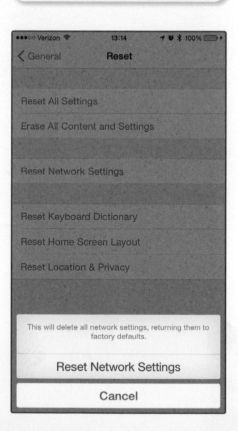

- **Weak signal?** Move closer to your router or Wi-Fi point and remember that brick walls, and other interferences can affect the signal.

- **Can you browse the web?** Launch a browser to test the web connection. Navigate to an easy-to-load page like google.co.uk.

- **Check your Wi-Fi network:** If the status bar shows you're connected but web content won't load, it suggests a problem with the Wi-Fi network you're using. If you're at home, check the cable connection to your Wi-Fi router or try connecting another device to the network to test it.

- **Reset network settings:** This will clear your 3G and Wi-Fi network settings, including saved networks, Wi-Fi passwords and VPN settings, so it is a last resort. Tap Settings > General and then scroll down and press Reset > Reset Network Settings. When the phone reboots, find and join the Wi-Fi network again.

Phone

If you're having trouble making or receiving calls

Left: Resetting network settings should be a last resort when solving connectivity problems.

and texts, try the following:

○ **Airplane Mode:** Swipe up on the Home screen to bring up the Control Centre and make sure the airplane icon is not lit.

○ **Signal:** In the top left-hand corner you'll see the signal bar. The more bars, the stronger the signal. If you're only seeing one or two bars, calls and texts might not work.

○ **Location:** If you're inside, head outside. Or, if you're already outside, chase that phone signal!

○ **Switch Airplane Mode on and off:** Go to Settings and toggle Airplane Mode on and then off. This resets your wireless data connections and can flush out any related problems.

○ **Restart your phone:** Yes, we know it's an old trick, but it often works.

○ **SIM card:** With your phone switched off, remove the SIM tray and take out the SIM card and reposition. Reinsert the tray and restart the phone.

○ **Restore your phone:** Still no joy? The next step is to restore your phone (*see* page 242 to find out how this is done).

Above: Check to see if you are connected to a Wi-Fi network quickly by looking at the Wi-Fi icon in the Command Center.

SYNCING

This section looks at problems that can occur while syncing your iPhone with iTunes and iCloud and any gremlins preventing your computer from recognizing the existence of your handset.

Above: Restart the phone by pressing and holding the power button, as indicated.

iTunes

When connecting your device to your computer – either via USB or Lightning connector for iOS devices purchased after September 2012 – an iPhone icon should appear in iTunes in the top menu. If this doesn't happen, then here is what you can do:

○ **Update iTunes**
○ **Restart your phone**
○ **Recharge your phone**
○ **Restart your computer**
○ **Uninstall and reinstall iTunes**

iTunes Syncing Over Wi-Fi

Since the launch of iTunes 10.5 (we're now on version 12), you can sync your iPhone with iTunes over the air and go fully computer-free. For this to

Hot Tip

Using iCloud rather than iTunes to sync and back up photos means that your pictures will be automatically updated when you join a Wi-Fi network (*see* page 42 for more iCloud benefits).

work, you'll need a device running iOS 5 or later and be connected to the same Wi-Fi network as your computer, which needs to be running iTunes 10.5 or later. If that's all present and correct and you're still having problems, there are some crucial checks you need to make:

- **Ensure Wi-Fi sync is enabled**
- **Quit iTunes and restart**
- **Restart your network router**
- **Check your network connection**
- **Check your firewall settings**

Not Enough Free Space

Whether you're syncing over Wi-Fi or via USB/Lightning, you might encounter the following message: 'iPhone cannot be synced because there is not enough free space to hold all of the items in the iTunes Library (additional space required)'. To fix this, try turning off the automatic syncing function in iTunes, as shown here:

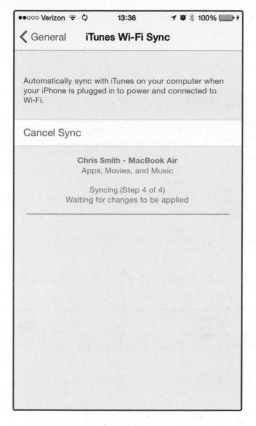

Above: You can sync content from your iTunes Library to your iPhone over Wi-Fi.

- **Select your iPhone**: In the iTunes navigation bar, find your iPhone and click the Summary tab.

- **Turn off Auto Sync**: Deselect Automatically sync when this iPhone is connected and select the Sync only ticked songs and videos tickbox. Click Apply: this will sync the changes to your iPhone.

Above: If you run out of free space, you should deselect the option to Automatically sync when this iPhone is connected. Instead, you should select the option to Sync only ticked songs and videos.

○ **Sync less data**: If syncing your entire music library exceeds the memory capacity of your iPhone, then choose Selected playlists to transfer rather than All songs and playlists under the Music tab in iTunes. You can also manage apps, films and iBooks in the same way.

Hot Tip

Having trouble syncing over Wi-Fi? Check that your iPhone is connected to the same Wi-Fi network as your Mac or PC, as it won't work if it isn't. Your iPhone will also need to be plugged into a power source.

iCLOUD

iCloud is great for backing up all of your favourite content and being able to access it from any Apple device (and some non-Apple devices), but it's also a complicated beast if it goes wrong. As there are far too many troubleshooting issues to cover here in detail, we'll show you how to spot and fix the most common troubles (also try apple.com/support/icloud).

> ### Hot Tip
> **Ensure you have at least 50 MB free space available on your iPhone before you attempt to back up. If you have no space available, iCloud Backup can fail.**

- **Can't sign into iCloud?** Make sure you're using the Apple ID email address you used when you set up your iCloud account. If you've forgotten your password, you can reset it online at appleid.apple.com.

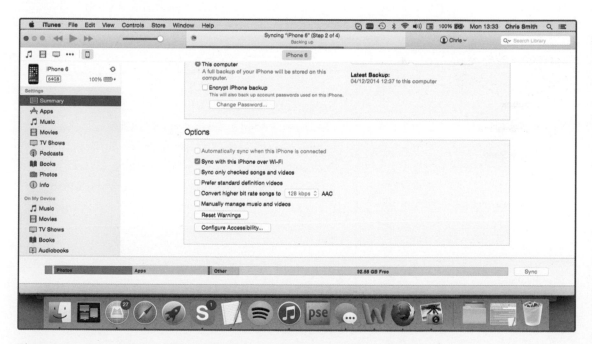

Above: You can check and adjust your backup settings through the Summary section of your iTunes account.

○ **Automatic backups won't start?** These only start when your iPhone is plugged into a power source, connected to Wi-Fi and the screen is locked. You can start a backup manually by tapping Back Up Now in Settings > iCloud > Storage & Backup.

○ **Out of cloud storage space?** If you're told you don't have enough cloud storage space, try excluding your Camera Roll and other large data items from backups. If that's not fixing the problem, you can always buy more storage to add to the free 5 GB provided by Apple.

Above: iCloud Drive allows you to access files on all of your Apple devices.

iCLOUD DRIVE

One of the reasons you may need more storage space is if you're using iCloud Drive. It is an online-based storage locker, which allows you to access any of your files on multiple Apple devices and at iCloud.com. If you don't have a Mac computer, it's not that much use, so you can probably skip this section.

Setting up iCloud Drive

Firstly, you'll need an iPhone running iOS 8 and a Mac computer running OS X Yosemite. If you do, head to Settings > iCloud and turn on iCloud Drive. On your Mac go to System Preferences > iCloud and tick the iCloud Drive. An iCloud Drive tab should now appear in your Finder Window.

Sharing Files to iCloud Drive

If you've ever used Dropbox, iCloud Drive works in the same way. The idea is that items saved to iCloud Drive will be synced across multiple devices, allowing you to work with one version that's accessible wherever you are. You can share any file as long as it's less than 15 GB in size, and it can be picked up on your iPhone in compatible programs like Pages, Numbers and Keynote.

Finding iCloud Drive Files

There's no iCloud Drive app on your iPhone (there probably should be), so in order to open a file, you'll need to go to the app you intend to open the file in. Let's use Pages, the document-creating tool. If you open Pages, you should see the file you shared right there. You can view and edit, and any changes will be automatically synced back to your Mac.

My Photos Are Not Appearing in My Photo Stream

From your iPhone's Home screen, select Settings > iCloud > Photos > My Photo Stream and make sure that the slider is on, then make sure that Wi-Fi is switched on and that you're connected to a wireless network. Photo Stream won't upload photos from an iOS device until the Camera app is closed on the device you used to take the photo, so check this. Also ensure your iPhone battery hasn't dropped below 20 per cent, as Photo Stream downloading and uploading are disabled when the battery reaches this threshold.

Above: You can check and adjust your Photo Stream settings.

APPS

Most of the apps in the App Store work well – most of the time. However, even the best-maintained apps can be prone to bugs; from crashing to sluggish performance, here's what to do when your apps aren't working:

Above: Multitasking screen showing which apps are live.

○ **Close the app:** If an app gets stuck during loading, you can bump-start it. Double-tap your phone's Home button to see a list of all open apps. Scroll to find the rogue app, then just swipe its card up off the screen and reopen the app as normal.

○ **Update the app:** Sometimes apps become glitchy because the developers have released an update. Go to App Store > Updates to check.

○ **Reset your iPhone:** Resetting fixes 95 per cent of glitches. Reset your phone by holding the Home and Power buttons simultaneously for 10 seconds and open the app again.

○ **Delete and reinstall the app:** Press down on the app icon until an x appears over it; press it and confirm you want to delete the app. Once it's gone, you can then reinstall it.

BATTERY

If your iPhone battery is winding up empty too quickly, you might have a faulty battery. However, it's more likely that your settings and usage are drinking more power than necessary. Here are some simple ways to make your iPhone last longer:

○ **Drain the battery:** About once a month, let the phone run until it shuts down on its own and then charge it back up to full.

○ **Close background apps:** Double-tap your phone's Home button to see a list of everything running in multitasking. Swipe each card up and off the screen to close it.

- **Push Notifications**:
  If lots of Push notifications are enabled, they can wear down your battery. Go to Settings > Notifications and click on the apps from which you don't need notifications. The Mail app is a particular culprit.

"Asphalt8" Would Like to Send You Notifications
Notifications may include alerts, sounds, and icon badges. These can be configured in Settings.

Don't Allow   OK

Above: Apps will often request permission to send you push notifications.

- **A weak 3G signal**:
  Your phone works harder when it's struggling to find a 3G signal. If you're going to be in an area with bad coverage for a long period, switch on Airplane Mode.

- **Turn off 4G LTE**: Using 4G internet is a bigger drain on the battery. Head to Settings > Cellular and toggle off the Enable LTE setting.

- **Adjust screen brightness**: Switch on the Auto-Brightness function in Settings > Display & Brightness settings and the iPhone will adjust itself, depending on light conditions.

- **Location Services**: If you don't need your location pinpointed, go to Settings > Location Services and choose which apps you want to use location.

- **Turn off Background App Refresh**: You can toggle individual apps through Settings > General > Background App Refresh.

○ **Turn Wi-Fi/Bluetooth off**: The constant search for Wi-Fi networks drains power. Newer iPhones use Bluetooth 4.0 which consumes less power, but it still has an impact.

○ **Update your iOS software**: Each version of iOS tends to deliver battery life improvements, so make sure you're running the latest version.

FROZEN iPHONE

iPhones freeze for a number of reasons. Closing a rogue app can get you going again. However, if your phone completely locks up, follow these simple steps to get it back up and running:

○ **Recharge**: Make sure your phone is fully charged. Turn it off while it's charging and use the mains charger. If a full battery doesn't cure the seizure, it's time to restart.

○ **Restart**: If this doesn't fix the problem, it's time to reset.

○ **Reset**: Resetting your iPhone is the equivalent of rebooting a crashed computer. It's a simple technique that shouldn't affect your data but can resolve a host of issues. Simply press and hold the Power button while simultaneously pressing and holding the Home button. You should see an Apple logo appear. After that, you can let go and your phone should restart.

○ **Restore**: Restoring your phone is not something you do lightly, but if you've tried the options above and all that has failed, then it might be your only option. Before you start, back up your phone if you can.

1. Connect your phone to your computer like you would if you were syncing.

2. When iTunes opens, select the Summary tab and click the Restore button.

3. Re-sync your phone to restore your data. You'll have to go through setup again and select from Restore from iTunes Backup or Restore from iCloud backup, depending on which you use.

○ **Recovery**: If recharging, restarting, resetting and restoring haven't fixed your fault, the final option is to put your phone into Recovery Mode.

1. If you have a Lightning or USB cable connected to your iPhone, disconnect it but leave the other end plugged into your computer. Turn off your iPhone by pressing the Power button and sliding the red slider.

2. Reconnect the Lightning or USB cable to your iPhone while simultaneously pressing and holding the Home button, and your iPhone should come on.

3. Keep holding the Home button and only release it when the Connect to iTunes screen appears. iTunes should launch automatically, but if it hasn't, open it manually.

4. Restore your phone following the steps in the Restore section (see opposite).

RUNNING OUT OF SPACE

Once you start downloading apps, games, music, films and photos, it's easy to fill up your iPhone's storage. There are many ways to manage your content more smartly to free up space.

Managing Storage Space
○ **Find out what's using your storage**
○ **Delete unused apps**
○ **Remove old videos**
○ **Back up your photos and videos shot using the iPhone's camera**. Once they're stored elsewhere (perhaps through iCloud Photo Library), you can delete them from the device without fear of losing them.

Above: Checking the Usage screen in General Settings can inform you what's taking up all your space.

MEMORY

In order to have your iPhone performing at its best, you need both RAM (random access memory) and free storage space. The way the iPhone is built means that you have fairly limited options for maximizing this, but here are a few things you can do.

INCREASING STORAGE SPACE

Unlike some smartphones, it's not possible to extend the iPhone's storage space with an external memory card. The only way to increase available space is to delete the apps you never use and remove old content you no longer need, such as videos and podcasts. You can manage this on the handset or via iTunes, but be aware: anything removed locally on the device will reappear unless you also remove it from your iTunes (see the section about managing storage space on page 243 to learn how).

Switch to Streaming

A great way to free up space on your iPhone is to switch to web-based options for music and video. You don't need to store all that iTunes music on your phone if you can stream it over Wi-Fi using an app like Spotify.

Above: You can close down apps by swiping them off screen in the multitasking view in order to speed up the performance of your iPhone.

SECURITY

The iPhone is an expensive piece of technology. Keeping the physical product safe is essential, but it's just as important to protect the data and information stored on your phone.

PROTECTION

Like most things techy, the iPhone allows you to set up a passcode so you can protect yourself and your information. Although it's another number or magic word to remember, it's advisable to assign a passcode, and if you're using an iPhone 5S/6/6 Plus, a Touch ID fingerprint too. It's easy to do and, should your phone fall into the wrong hands, you'll be thankful you did.

Passcode Lock

You should have set this up when we set up the phone, but if not, you can set a password to prevent unscrupulous people from unlocking your phone. Go into Settings > Touch ID & Passcode and enter a four-digit code. You'll be asked to verify the code to ensure it matches.

Increased-security Passcode

If you want to set a more complex passcode, you can switch off Simple Passcode. You'll then get the option of assigning a longer password that combines numbers, letters and special characters.

Above: You can choose your own passcode to increase security.

Failed Passcode Data Dump

From the same Settings menu, you can set the iPhone to automatically Erase Data if someone makes 10 failed attempts at unlocking your phone with the passcode. Be warned: all your media, data, settings and information will be deleted, so think carefully before you activate this.

Touch ID

Within the same menu, you can add a digit that'll enable you to unlock your phone with a fingerprint. We explained this earlier in the book when setting up

Right: Setting up an additional Touch ID fingerprint can be useful if more than one member of your household uses the device.

●●○○○ Verizon	13:51	🚀 🔋 ☀ 100% 🔋
❮ General	**Auto-Lock**	

1 Minute	
2 Minutes	✓
3 Minutes	
4 Minutes	
5 Minutes	
Never	

Above: Keeping the Auto-Lock time short ensures your phone is quickly secured.

the phone. Here, you can add more digits (if you share the device, for example) and also decide whether you want to use Touch ID to authorize iTunes and App Store purchases too.

Auto-Lock

To make your phone lock itself if it has been sitting idle, go into Settings > General > Auto-Lock and you can set the amount of time that elapses since your phone was last used before it automatically locks the display. Your options range from five minutes down to one minute. Selecting Never will quickly drain your battery.

SIM Locking

Any data that might be stored on your SIM card – anything from phone numbers to photos – can also be protected with a PIN code. Go to Settings > Phone and turn on SIM PIN and enter a password; this will prevent anyone else from using it in another phone without knowing the magic code.

Restrictions

The iPhone's restrictions tools let you dictate what can and can't be done with your phone. From locking the Safari web browser to preventing new apps being loaded on to the device, it's possible to manage the phone in a way that adds layers of safety, security and parental guidance. Head to Settings > General > Restrictions to create a Restrictions Passcode, then you can turn off access to certain apps and certain iTunes content (such as music with explicit lyrics).

ENCRYPTING BACKUP

Whenever you connect your iPhone to iTunes to sync, update or restore your device, most of your essential data is backed up to your computer's hard drive or to iCloud. This includes photos, text messages, notes, contact favourites and some settings. It's possible to keep this data safe from unwanted prying eyes by encrypting your backups for an added level of security.

Above: You can choose to encrypt your iPhone data by selecting the Encrypt iPhone backup option from the menu in the iTunes summary tab.

Encrypt Your Data

If you choose to back up your iPhone to your computer, you get the option to encrypt and password-protect your data. It's simple to do. Just connect your handset to your computer and open iTunes. Load the iPhone and in the summary section, click Back up to This computer and tick the box that says Encrypt iPhone backup.

VPN

A VPN, or Virtual Private Network, is most commonly used to provide secure access to a company's network behind a firewall. A VPN creates an encrypted internet connection that acts as a safe channel for sending and receiving data. You're most likely to have encountered this when sending emails on your work account from a phone outside of the office.

Setting up a VPN on Your iPhone

Setting up a Virtual Private Network is one of those things that sounds more complicated than it is. However, if you can get it, we'd advise seeking help from your company's IT experts. If you can't get help, at the very least, you'll need them to provide some key information before you start, including which protocol to use and the main configuration settings. If you're flying solo, once you're in possession of those vitals, here's what to do:

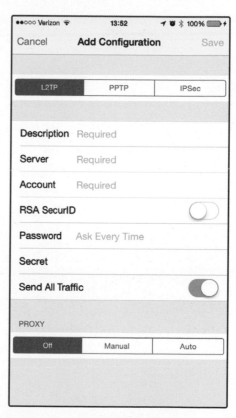

Above: You can set up a VPN on your iPhone.

- **Hit Settings and go to General > VPN:** Select Add VPN Configuration.

- **Choose the protocol:** You'll be asked to select which VPN protocol you wish to use. Choose: L2TP, PPTP or IPSec VPN.

- **Fill in the form:** Much of the setup is filling in boxes. Enter the server information, account details, password and encryption level (if one has been provided) – plus any other details you've been given by your IT people.

- **Switching a VPN on or off:** Once the initial setup is complete, you can toggle VPN on or off as you wish, via Settings.

TOP 100 APPS

This is our list of the top 100 apps we think that every iPhone user should have, or aspire to have. Some are essentials; others are those that you might use only occasionally but are what brings your iPhone to life. Have a look through our picks and see what your iPhone is missing out on.

Shopping

1. **eBay:** Sell or buy and find out instantly when a bid has been successful. **Free.**

2. **Amazon Mobile:** Use the iPhone camera to take a picture of a product to see if it's in stock. **Free.**

3. **Tesco:** The supermarket chain's app lets you do the shopping on the move. **Free.**

4. **RedLaser:** Use a barcode scanner to check the prices of items to discover where you can get them cheaper elsewhere. **Free.**

5. **Groupon:** Get special offers on experiences and events, depending on your current location. **Free.**

6. **Starbucks:** Pay for your coffee wirelessly with your digital Starbucks card and save towards rewards. **Free.**

7. **PayPal:** Send money, make payments, check your account details and more. **Free.**

Connectivity

8. **WhatsApp:** The multi-platform messaging app which allows you to freely chat with friends over the internet. **£0.79 per year.**

9. **Chrome:** Supports unlimited tabs and can send pages from your computer to your iPhone. **Free.**

10. **Mailbox:** An innovative email application, which enables Gmail users to get to 'Inbox zero'.

11. **Skype:** Make free voice calls, video conversations and instant messaging. **Free.**

12. **FaceTime:** Apple's video calling app uses the iPhone's front-facing camera. **Free.**

Watch and Listen

13. **Podcasts:** Download, subscribe and listen to your favourite podcasts.

14. **Sky Go:** Sky subscribers can watch both live and on-demand content. **Free.**

15. **BBC iPlayer:** Catch up on BBC TV programmes and radio. **Free.**

16. **4oD:** Channel 4's TV on-demand service lets you catch up with their shows. **Free.**

17. **Sky+:** Change your iPhone into a touch-screen remote control. **Free.**

18. **Virgin TV Anywhere:** Virgin TiVo customers can watch live TV over a Wi-Fi connection. **Free.**

19. **Movies by Flixster:** Get your local movie showtimes, buy tickets, check reviews, watch trailers and more. **Free.**

20. **Netflix:** Pay a monthly subscription and watch TV shows and films in full HD.

21. **Amazon Prime Instant Video:** Amazon Prime members can choose from over 70,000 TV shows and movies from the US and the UK.

Free

22. **Apple Remote:** Take control of iTunes or Apple TV and select playlists or adjust volume. **Free.**

23. **YouTube:** Browse and watch millions of videos from the most popular video sharing site in the world. **Free.**

24. **TV Guide.co.uk:** Check out what's on with up to date accurate TV listings. **Free.**

25. **Spotify:** Premium subscribers stream music over mobile data and Wi-Fi, and save playlists offline without being connected to the internet. **Free.**

26. **TuneIn Radio:** With access to over 60,000 global radio stations, you can pause live streams to re-listen to favourite shows. **Free.**

27. **iPlayer Radio:** The iPlayer for audio, it has access to 300 UK radio stations including your favourite BBC stations. **Free.**

28. **Shazam:** Hold the Shazam app up to a song and it will tell you all you need to know about the track. **Free.**

Reading

29. **The Guardian:** Offering access to the latest content from the British newspaper. **Free.**

30. **Newsstand:** Subscribe to digital newspapers and magazines, and the latest issues will be added to the virtual shelf **Free**

31. **Feedly:** This attractive RSS reader aggregates all of your favourite stories from around the web in one place. **Free.**

32. **BBC News:** Access content from one of the world's most reputable news services. **Free.**

33. **Instapaper:** Collect news stories from RSS feeds and the web; they will be stripped down so they are easier to read. **Free.**

34. **Pocket:** Pocket syncs to your device so you can catch up on articles when it is convenient. **Free.**

35. **iBooks:** Apple's official ebook store lets you buy and read a variety of books. **Free.**

36. **Kindle:** Read Kindle books, newspapers and magazines on your iPhone. **Free.**

Social Media

37. **Snapchat:** Messaging app that allows you to quickly share photos and videos that disappear within a set timeframe. Popular among younger iPhone users. **Free.**

38. **Facebook:** The friend-collecting site will let you update your status, check your news feed and receive notifications of posts. **Free.**

39. **Twitter:** Tweet on the go with the new Discover feature helping find suitable tweets and people to follow. **Free.**

40. **LinkedIn:** Giving you access to your entire professional network. **Free.**

41. **Beamly:** Combining social networking with live TV, view additional content about programmes and share comments. **Free.**

42. **Twitterific:** An alternative way to enjoy Twitter, if you get bored with the official app.

43. **Tumblr:** A great app for following your favourite blogs, sharing content and posting to your own. **Free.**

44. **Flipboard – Your Social Magazine:** Turn customizable news stories and social networking updates into a glossy magazine. **Free.**

Photos and Video

45. **Hipstamatic:** Produce retro-looking Polaroid-style photos with your iPhone. **£0.69.**

46. **Instagram:** Add filters to photographs to give them a vintage look, and share with other users via Facebook or Twitter. **Free.**

47. **Vine:** Record multiple clips and create entertaining, interesting six-second video loops. **Free.**

48. **Adobe Photoshop Express:** Includes many of the creative tools in the desktop version to modify and enhance images. **Free.**

49. **Dropbox:** Access files wherever you are, as well as offline, upload video and photos in bulk. **Free.**

50. **Pinterest:** Create boards and 'pin' images from the web to show the world what inspires you. **Free.**

51. **Flickr:** The photo-sharing app that now supports video will let you upload multiple content. **Free.**

52: **iMovie:** Edit and stitch together video clips, add captions and a soundtrack and upload the finished article to YouTube. **Free.**

53. **Moonpig:** Upload photos from your iPhone to create a unique card that can then be sent to the desired address. **Free.**

Geo-Location and Travel

54. **Google Maps:** If you're not happy with Apple Maps, you can download Google Maps and access great features like Street View. **Free.**

55. **Find My Friends:** Locate contacts with an iPhone, iPad or other Apple device to make meeting up easier. **Free.**

56. **Google Earth:** Search places from around the world with detailed maps. **Free.**

57. **The Night Sky:** Using the iPhone compass and GPS, hold the app up towards the sky to identify stars and constellations. **£0.69.**

58. **Dark Sky:** The most attractive, awesome weather app you're ever likely to see. It'll let you know the conditions up to an hour in advance. **£2.49.**

59. **Trip Advisor:** Offers a complete offline guide to cities, with visitor attraction details. **Free.**

60. **Flight Track:** You can check the status of your flight: real-time departures, gate closing times and alternative flights. **£2.99.**

61. **Skyscanner:** Find affordable flights covering over 1,000 airlines and purchase the ticket directly through the app. **Free.**

62. **British Airways:** Flying with BA? You can check flight information and use your iPhone as a boarding pass. **Free.**

63. **The Trainline:** Check live train times, view your next train home and buy tickets. **Free.**

64. **Odeon:** This app will help you find your nearest Odeon cinema and the films being shown. **Free.**

Sport and Fitness

65. **Apple Health:** The built-in Health app within iOS 8 will count steps and bring in data from various fitness tracking devices. **Free.**

66. **Endomondo:** One of the best apps, for keeping tabs on your workout information. **Free.**

67. **Runkeeper:** Track your running and cycling activity, see your route on a map and get information on distance and calories burned. **Free.**

68. **Johnson & Johnson:** Official seven minute workout: The workout you can perform at your desk on your break. All you need is a chair. **Free.**

69: **miCoach:** Prescribing training plans for different sports, GPS-based pace zones will help to push you further. **Free.**

70. **Instant Heart Rate:** Place your index finger on the iPhone camera to read your pulse. **£0.79.**

71. **Pact:** Wager real money on whether you'll go to the gym and watch your motivation soar. **Free.**

Games

72. **Candy Crush Saga:** The hit iPhone game of 2014 encourages you to swipe away candy patterns to complete levels. **Free.**

73. **Temple Run:** The reaction-style adventure game tests your ability to avoid obstacles at speed as you are chased by a gang of angry apes. **Free.**

74. **Cut the Rope:** Get the candy into the Om Nom monster by cutting ropes in this addictive puzzler. **Free.**

75. **Plants vs Zombies 2:** Build up your defences with weapon-firing greenery to protect against armies of marauding zombies reaching your front door. **Free.**

76. **Angry Birds:** Take out all of the pigs by flinging birds with different abilities from a slingshot in this massive mobile hit. **Free.**

77. **The Room:** A suspenseful strategy game, which requires you to unlock puzzles in order to discover supernatural mysteries. **Free.**

78. **Minecraft: Pocket Edition:** The open world-building game allows you to build up the world in your own image. **£4.99.**

Food and Restaurants

79. **Untappd:** Log your favourite beers from around the world, connect with friends and earn badges. **Free.**

80. **Jamie's Recipes:** The Naked Chef gives you the opportunity to subscribe to his latest recipes, packed with photos, videos and helpful tips. **Free.**

81. **Nigella's Quick Collection:** The gastronomic guide includes 70 recipes covering the best comfort foods and video tips of difficult meals. **£3.99.**

82. **Yell:** Find local restaurants, get directions and read reviews from recent patrons. **Free.**

83. **Big Oven:** Over 250,000 recipes searchable by keyboard. You can enter ingredients you have left in your pantry and see what the app comes up with. **Free.**

84. **Kitchen Pad Timer:** Timers display oven and stove temperatures with an alert to remind you when to take something out. **£1.49.**

To-Do List

85. **Evernote:** Take care of all note-taking from simple to-do lists to recording voice memos, all can be shared and accessed from evernote.com. **Free.**

86. **Task:** Simple yet sophisticated to-do list application, which makes it easier to plan your days. **£0.69.**

87. **Wunderlist:** One of the most attractive and usable to-do list apps on the App Store. **Free.**

Reference and Productivity

88. **Microsoft Office:** Access, create, edit and share Word, PowerPoint and Excel documents. **Free.**

89. **Google Search:** The stand-alone Google Search app for iPhone gives access to Google Now notifications, voice searches, maps, information and more. **Free.**

90. **Google Translate:** Translate phrases, sentences and words into over 60 languages after you have either typed them or spoken into your phone. **Free.**

91. **IMDb Movies and TV:** Comprehensive source of information about every film and TV show ever made. **Free.**

92. **Wikipanion:** Wikipanion remembers where you last left a Wikipedia page and keeps a history of all the pages you've searched for previously. **Free.**

93. **Dragon Dictation:** Siri does this also, but Dragon allows you to dictate messages and emails to your phone using voice. **Free.**

94. **Swype:** Making texting a speedier process, swipe across the keyboard to make words with predictive dictionary support to aid accuracy. **£0.79.**

95: **GarageBand:** Create music on your iPhone using a range of digital instruments. **Free.**

Finances

96. **Coin Keeper Classic:** Monitor your finances by seeing how much you spend, tracking expenses and setting weekly budgets. **£3.99.**

97. **1password:** Creates strong, unique passwords for every site, remembers them all for you, and logs you in with a single tap. It also has Touch ID integration. **Free.**

Useful Stuff

98. **UK Postage Calculator:** Get the right stamps on packages and letters by calculating the price depending on weight and the destination. **£1.99.**

99. **iHandy Level Free:** This app can turn the iPhone into a spirit level as well as other DIY tools, such as a pendulum and a ruler. **Free.**

100. **XE.com:** Quickly access the latest currency exchange rates on your iPhone. **Free.**

INDEX